RAISING
RABBITS
THE
MODERN
WAY

Bob Bennett

A Garden Way Publishing Book

Storey Communications, Inc.
Pownal Vermont 05261

DEDICATION
TO MY MOTHER, who helped me to start right, and
TO MY WIFE, who has encouraged me to continue.

Printed in the United States by
Capital City Press
Fifteenth Printing, June 1985

Library of Congress Cataloging in Publication Data

Bennett, Bob, 1936-
  Raising rabbits the modern way.

  Bibliography: p.
  Includes index.
  1. Rabbits.   I. Title
SF453.B46   636'.93'22   75-31601
ISBN 0-88266-067-5

Contents

Introduction

Twenty-five years ago, as a boy in Vermont, I started raising rabbits right because Anthony Pisanelli had my best interests at heart. He made sure I began with good rabbits! My backyard hutches produced many rabbits, spending-money and time left over to spend it, not to mention a few dollars extra to put in the bank. I also won a Boy Scout merit badge in the bargain, plus a trophy and a few ribbons. And the fried rabbit dinners are unforgettable! Mr. Pisanelli is still starting people right with rabbits. Retired now, he has more time than ever to raise rabbits and, moreover, runs the absolute *best* rabbit shows I ever attended.

Fifteen years after Tony got me going, after college, military service and apartment life, I returned to my boyhood pursuit of rabbit raising in the backyard, and at this writing am happily hot at it. And so, after raising the animals myself and watching others try it with varying results, I'm prompted to pass along the newer ways I have learned to house, feed, breed, show and sell rabbits right. In this book, I show you how to do all this (and more) by starting right and doing it the modern way too!

Of course, one way to begin is to keep reading. Another way is to join the American Rabbit Breeders Association immediately. After serving ARBA for several years as its publicity chairman, and after founding and editing the association's *Domestic Rabbits* magazine. I have learned that this association is a marvelous one and has a lot to offer *all* rabbit raisers, beginners and advanced.

So if you want to start raising rabbits the modern way, read this book — and *join* the ARBA!

ACKNOWLEDGMENTS

I am very grateful to the following persons for their support and encouragement: Anthony Pisanelli; Robert Noble; Charles Lyons; Charles Maurer; Frank Miglis; Robert Densmore; Ted, Flo Ann, and Tammy Gordon; James Blyth; John Dack; Frank DelMastro; Pat Schmidt; H. John Nelson; Oren Reynolds; Robert Dubbell; Edward Peifer; Edward Stahl; Bill Dorn; Paul Posel; J. Calvin Downing, D.V.M.; Jerry Belanger; Sam Mines; H. Joseph Hull; and Ron Epstein.

Sincere thanks go to each individual and organization for information and illustrations used here. Particularly helpful were Pel-Freez, Favorite Manufacturing, and, of course, John Dack.

At Garden Way Publishing, I am indebted to Edward Miller and Walter Hard, Jr., my editors, whose helpful suggestions improved the manuscript.

I would also like to thank the hundreds of members of the American Rabbit Breeders Association, the New Jersey Rabbit Breeders Association, and the Green Mountain Rabbit Breeders Association who, over the years, have contributed much that found its way into this book.

BOB BENNETT
October, 1975

PHOTO CREDITS

Favorite Manufacturing Co., Box 176B, New Holland, PA 17557: pp. 16, 48, 49, 52, 79

Pel-Freez: pp 17, 134

Ralston Purina Co., Checkboard Square, St. Louis, MO 63188: p. 59

Ted Gordon: pp. 13, 32, 106

All other photos by the author

1
Why Start?

Take one look at the domestic rabbit and you will understand its appeal. Recognize it as an animal that thrives almost anywhere, is inexpensive to obtain and easy to maintain. Add its legendary prolificacy, unmatched cleanliness and a steadfast refusal to bark at the moon at midnight or crow at the neighbors at 6 a.m. Consider, above all, its versatility and you will comprehend readily its steadily zooming popularity.

When I think of versatility, I'm reminded of a fanciful creature that was born in the comic strips in the late 1940s. You may recall it was then that Li'l Abner creator Al Capp introduced the Shmoo, a prolific and lovable little animal that was perfectly willing to be anything anyone in Dogpatch desired. If Daisy Mae wanted pork chops or steak, ice cream or cake, the Shmoo immediately multiplied and became a two-legged movable feast like manna from heaven. He obliged. And so warmed by this accommodating versatility was faddish America that toy Shmoos appeared in novelty stores across the land.

But while the Shmoo was only the figment of a lively imagination, it easily could have been inspired by the rabbit, a prolific and lovable little creature that actually is many of the things the Shmoo could be.

FIRST OF ALL, GOOD EATING

Above all, the domestic rabbit produced in backyards and in commercial rabbitries is mighty good to eat. It can be prepared and served in so many tempting ways that even Daisy Mae would favor it over the Shmoo. But the accommodating rabbit also serves daily in medical research, and as mittens, muffs, toys, novelties, hats, collars, cuffs and coats. And gardeners beg for the manure, which boasts some unique properties that benefit flowers and vegetables alike.

The all-white, fine-grained meat of the domestic rabbit finds its way to supermarket frozen food counters as packaged, cut-up, 2½ pound fryer-broilers, at a price competitive with beef. But rabbit meat equals or exceeds beef, pork, lamb and chicken in protein content, and has a lower percentage of fat, less cholesterol and fewer calories than the competition. Delicious hot or cold, fancy or plain, it can be breaded and fried, broiled, baked or barbecued. Larger rabbits are roasted according to many recipes developed over the years in this country and abroad. Because of the fine bones and the fact that they carry a lot of fine-grained meat, a small portion of rabbit goes a long way. For example, you will fill up faster on rabbit than on an equal portion of chicken.

COMMERCIAL BREEDERS IN THE OZARKS

In the United States, the area of northern Arkansas and southern Missouri contains about 1,500 breeders of meat rabbits. They range from backyard producers to full-time commercial operators who serve the nation's largest processing plant, operated by the Pel-Freez Company at Rogers, Arkansas.

While this area, generally known as the Ozarks, boasts the greatest concentration of rabbit producers in the country, many thousands more are scattered throughout the United States. An independent research company estimated a total United States annual production of live weight rabbit meat at 34.2 million pounds in the mid-1970s. Because the rabbit normally is marketed at a weight of four pounds, this amounts to almost 8.5 million rabbits produced each year for consumption on American tables.

A FAVORITE IN EUROPE

But United States production and consumption of rabbits lags far behind that of Europe, where Italy, Germany, France and Spain are the world's biggest producers and most willing consumers. British production and consumption figures equal those of the United States but give the Britons a much higher per capita consumption rate.

Europeans and the British eat a lot more rabbit than Americans do because wherever land is at a premium, the rabbit shines. One doe, in one hutch, can produce 70 to 95 pounds of dressed, edible meat each year — about nine times her own live weight. In America, where plenty of land is still available to plant corn for hogs and to graze cattle, rabbit raising has not gained as much attention as it has in the Old World. But as land for livestock becomes increasingly scarce, it stands to reason that rabbits will become more popular here.

RABBITS SERVE SCIENCE

Another significant use of rabbits is in the scientific sector. About two million are utilized in United States medical and pharmaceutical laboratories each year. Most of these rabbits are raised in the Delaware-Maryland-Virginia (Delmarva) area and in Pennsylvania, New York, New Jersey and Massachusetts. But many are trucked up to the Northeast from the Ozarks to meet the demand.

Adding the meat and laboratory production figures together, you might surmise that there is a total United States rabbit population of about 10.5 million. But that figure would exclude those in the hutches of thousands of fanciers who raise rabbits mainly for exhibition. It is also exclusive of those who supply the meat and laboratory producers.

THE FANCIERS' ROLE

Basic to the acceptance of meat and laboratory rabbits is the availability of quality, well-bred stock. This is provided by the fanciers, who guard carefully the purity of the pedigrees of more than 50 recognized varieties, which range from 20 pound giants to two-pound dwarfs famous for popping out of magicians' hats. These fanciers and some commercial growers hold membership in the American Rabbit Breeders Association, Inc., which maintains a national headquarters in Bloomington, Illinois. In addition to supplying choice breeding stock required by profit-conscious commercial growers, they also supply some meat and laboratory specimens and compete in hundreds of fairs and special exhibitions, including a week-long annual convention that moves to a different location each year. They also belong to hundreds of state and county breeders associations, as well as national breed specialty clubs dedicated to their favorite kind of rabbit. They read scores of national, regional and local trade and association publications, most of which are produced by volunteers from among their own ranks. They also read *Domestic Rabbits* magazine, which is the only nationally circulated magazine devoted exclusively to rabbits. *Domestic Rabbits* is the official publication of the ARBA, and is issued to the entire membership six times a year.

WOULD YOU BELIEVE 12 MILLION RABBITS?

At last count, ARBA membership rolls numbered nearly 20,000 adults and youngsters, which was up from only 8,000 members merely five years previously. In the preceding decade that began in 1960, the membership increased only a couple of thousand or so.

There doubtless are an additional hundred thousand unidentified backyard rabbit raisers with no affiliation whatsoever. In my county in New Jersey, for example, there are at least half a dozen small raisers who do not belong to the ARBA for every one who does. I'd estimate, therefore, the existence of about 12 million rabbits in the United States. This is a conservative guess but nevertheless a lot of rabbits — even for rabbits.

HERE'S WHERE YOU COME IN

After this brief review of the scope of the rabbit industry, it is perfectly appropriate for you to inquire where you fit into the picture. For the answer, ask yourself why, in fact, you should raise rabbits at all.

One reason might be the simple joy of the miracle of living things, and their companionship, and the pleasure of meeting their needs. You might raise them like so many pretty flowers and simply enjoy watching them bloom. Many successful rabbit raisers need no further reason for keeping their hutches filled with beautiful rabbits. And keeping them filled, for them, is proof of their success. In fact, I know no successful rabbit raiser who does not raise rabbits for at *least* this reason, although some will not admit it.

You might be more practical (if you're like me) and demand utility as well as beauty. So you might propagate rabbits for a pair of warm, furry mittens, a delectable dish on the table, a gleaming trophy in the showroom — even college tuition for your children, a roof over your head or money in the bank.

Good reasons abound, but a few are bad. I'll explain some of the latter later, but you should know about one of them as soon as possible. The worst reason to raise rabbits is to get rich quick. Beware of the fly-by-night operators who advertise schemes with a promise that you will get rich quick! Later on I'll tell you more about these predators-in-rabbit-fur who are doubtless the biggest blots on the rabbit scene. In the meantime, I'll promise you this about them: they will only get you *poor* quick!

Many Americans have achieved success with rabbits, because the rabbit has so much going for it. But it is perhaps precisely because it seems to some easy to raise rabbits that many who try fail in discouragement in a very short time. One vital aspect lies hidden beneath that soft and furry exterior — the necessity for starting right. I know rabbit raisers who have achieved success in only a few months.

Others still seek it after many years, and if they hang on to old misguided notions, they never will succeed.

RABBITS THE MODERN WAY

This book probably owes its existence more to *progress* in rabbit raising than to anything else. Previous books on the subject were written before recent, more modern methods of housing, feeding and managing rabbits were devised. Authors of books on the subject often advocated home construction of hutches from shipping crates, nail kegs and prohibitively expensive lumber. You will find no such recommendations on these pages. Today, the rabbit raiser has at his disposal a broad line of equipment especially designed for the animals. Today, complete pelleted feed containing every nutritional element required by the rabbit is readily available everywhere in the country (and the city). No longer must producers risk formulating their own feeds. No longer must they fool with mixed grains and possibly moldy greens in an effort to find a feed that will put meat on their stock without making them sick and even killing them.

You who start raising rabbits now have everything in your favor — feed, equipment, medication and, especially, *sound advice!* The way has been cleared for you by others, but the most important step remains, and only *you* can take it. Put your foot down! Say that *this thing is worth doing well.* Make that kind of commitment and I guarantee you will follow in the footsteps of those who have started right and are raising rabbits the modern way.

2
The Right Rabbit

The best way to start right with rabbits is to start with the right rabbit. Which is the right rabbit for you?

Approximately 50 individual breeds and varieties of domestic rabbits are recognized by the American Rabbit Breeders Association. This domestic rabbit that is available in so many sizes, shapes and colors is not a wild animal, but a domesticated farm species. It's not a rodent, either, but a *lagomorph,* a gnawing mammal of a different order. It is well to keep these two characteristics in mind because these popular misconceptions keep surfacing periodically and create resistance to the rabbit. People must be reminded that they will not be eating a stringy, tough, wild game animal that must be chewed cautiously while spitting out birdshot. Nor is the rabbit a rat.

SPECIES 40 MILLION YEARS OLD

The rabbit was domesticated several centuries ago. It might have happened first in Africa, Spain, France, Belgium or in Rome, depending upon which report you read. I have come across several such accounts without really doing any research on the subject, and, frankly, I don't know which, if any, to believe. It is said that wild rabbits were used for food in Asia at least 3,000 years ago. Geologists claim to have proved that rabbits and opossums are the oldest known living animals and date back 30 or 40 million years. Spanish caves contain pictures of rabbits. A sphinx built in Turkey about 1,500 B.C. has been standing on the figures of two rabbits for about 3,500 years.

The Easter Bunny legend descends from the Teutons. According to one account, a goddess changed a bird into a rabbit which was understandably so appreciative of this miraculous metamorphosis, that when the goddess scheduled her spring festival, it laid colored eggs for the occasion. My four-year-old daughter still inquires about this. Imagine a rabbit that could lay eggs. It boggles the mind!

The use of rabbit feet as good luck charms dates to the following old superstition: the left hind foot of a rabbit taken into a churchyard at midnight when the moon is full will shield its owner from evil. I for one have never believed this. I mean, how much did it do for its original owner? I confess, however, to remaining absent from church-yards on clear evenings.

An entire book could be written about rabbit lore and legend, but that's not the purpose of the one you hold in your hands. The account would have to include the current Playboy nonsense, which personally I rather despise, although I remind those who ask about the rabbit's prolificacy that, after all, it does get its picture on the cover of that national magazine every month.

IT'S PROBABLY NOT A BELGIAN HARE

Domestic rabbits probably were raised before the Belgian Hare boom at the beginning of this century, but that's when rabbit keeping really took off in the United States. I know people who still refer to all domestic rabbits as *Belgian Hares* (it's not a hare, a closely related wild species, but a rabbit), although the Belgian actually is a somewhat obscure breed in the United States today.

Probably the most important development in the history of domestic rabbits in this country happened in 1913 when the New Zealand Red arrived on these shores. Reds were brought to the Pacific Coast by sailors who obtained them in New Zealand, where they were that country's natural wild rabbits and also performed as a commercial animal. A lot more history of rabbits can be found if you are so inclined, but the task at hand is to build your future with rabbits. So it is probably sufficient to say that the 50 kinds of rabbits we have today were carefully (sometimes accidentally) developed for specific purposes by fanciers.

THE RIGHT RABBIT FOR THE RIGHT PURPOSE

What remains, therefore, is for you to identify your purpose and the best breed for you. The single most important step you will take toward starting right is to address yourself to this question: What am I going to do with my rabbits?

To answer, let's categorize the many breeds by weight and fur type. Then, let's take a look at the markets for them. Remember, success in rabbit raising demands that you produce more rabbits than you are able to house. Even if you merely raise them for the purest of motives — only to have them around — you will simply have to dispose of some. More practically, the producer of show stock must make room for younger, improved animals. Those who produce breeding stock, meat, laboratory and even pet stock must meet certain production goals. If they are bred for home consumption, you will want to keep the freezer stocked.

All of the various breeds fall into four categories by weight. You'll find photos of some breeds and all weight classes in this book.

THE GIANTS — A BIT TOO BIG?

Appropriately, the largest rabbits are called the giants. Among them are the *Flemish Giant,* the world's largest rabbit, which weighs up

The Giant Chinchillas weigh up to 15 pounds.

to 20 pounds; and the *Giant Chinchilla* and the *Checkered Giant,* which weigh 12 to 15 pounds. Some producers of meat rabbits raise the giant breeds, but most do not. They prefer those in the medium weight range. Big is not necessarily better. The giants' bones and appetites rival their size so their feed/meat conversion capacity makes them less profitable than the medium breeds.

MIDDLEWEIGHTS — ON TARGET

Medium weight rabbits reach 9 to 12 pounds at maturity. Among the most popular are the New Zealand Whites, Californians, Satins and Champagne D'Argents. Meat producers like this group because they shoot for a meaty, fine-boned fryer weighing four pounds or more at eight weeks of age. Medium weight rabbits come closest to that target.

A Champagne D'Argent   Californian is a middleweight, too.

THERE'S A PLACE FOR THE LITTLE ONES

Small rabbits include, besides the Tan and the Dutch, the English Spot, the Havana and others. These weigh 4-7 pounds, are popular as exhibition animals and have considerable utility value as meat and in the laboratory.

Barely nudging the scales at a mere mature weight of 2-3 pounds are the Netherland Dwarf, the Polish, and a relative newcomer to our shores, the Britannia Petite. These rabbits displace hamsters, gerbils and guinea pigs. If you want rabbits and lack space, these are for you.

*A Netherland
Dwarf*

NORMAL FUR

Normal-furred rabbits dominate the species. You will find examples in each weight group; including the Flemish Giant, New Zealand, Tan and Netherland Dwarf, among others. Normal fur is about an inch long. Good normal fur returns quickly to its natural position and lies smoothly over the body when stroked toward the rabbit's head. The under fur is fine, soft and dense.

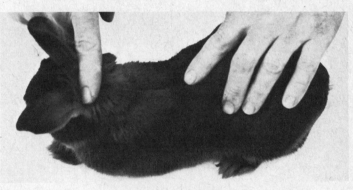

Dense, soft coat of normal-furred rabbit lies flat.

REX FUR

Rex fur is worn, naturally, by Rex rabbits, which are in the medium weight group only. Short and plushlike, Rex fur stands upright and has guard hairs almost as short as the undercoat. Rex fur is only about 5/8 of an inch long.

Opal Rex has plush-like fur.

Red Satin wears a lustrous coat.

SATIN FUR

Extremely popular are the Satins, which come in a wide range of colors. All are in the medium weight class. Satin fur consists of a small diameter hair shaft and a more transparent hair shell than is displayed by the normal-furred breeds. This greater transparency of the outer hair shell gives the Satin fur more intense color and more luster compared to the normal-furred breeds, with the exception of the Tan, whose luster is unsurpassed. Satin fur is about an inch long, about the same as normal fur.

Angoras are raised for their long wool.

ANGORA WOOL

We can more properly describe the coat of the Angora rabbit as wool. Angoras, small-to-medium size rabbits, appear quite large because of their fluffy wool coats. The length of the wool is about three inches, so there is no mistaking the Angora; you will know him when you see him.

With the exception of the Angora, rabbits are not raised primarily for their coats. Fur is a by-product of the meat rabbit, and because Americans prefer a young, fryer-broiler rabbit, the fur is immature and unsuitable for garments. At various times there has been a market for fryer fur as felt to the hat trade, because felt hats often have been in fashion. Since President John F. Kennedy decided to go hatless, however, hats have mostly been out for men and the women seem to have doffed theirs, too. This market is unpredictable to say the least. The rabbit fur coats worn by the ladies and some men generally are made from the fur of the European rabbits because Europeans prefer a roaster rabbit that wears a mature, prime coat. So the Europeans have cornered the commercial garment market. If you see a coat advertised as being made of "French rabbit" it doesn't mean that France has better rabbits than anybody else. It means simply that the French will butcher a 10 pound rabbit for the table in mid-winter when the hide is mature, thick and prime. In this country there is little such fur available.

In the case of Angora wool, demand is slight and payment poor. Therefore, fur and wool offer little in the way of markets in themselves. By that I mean you probably wouldn't find it worthwhile to produce rabbits mainly for the coats they wear. On the other hand, you certainly can make something from them and you might be ingenious enough to turn them into your prime source of income, as far as your rabbitry is concerned. Some have and so can you. We'll take a closer look at this in Chapter 7.

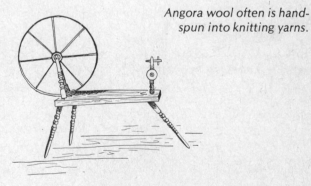

Angora wool often is hand-spun into knitting yarns.

FIRST YOUR MARKET, THEN YOUR BREED

Right now, however, the next best thing to say is that you simply must pick your purpose or your market *before* you pick your breed. You might surmise that I recommend you raise only one breed for only one purpose — and you are almost right. Most breeds, however, will serve more than one purpose.

Meat, laboratory and breeding stock — these are the major uses for rabbits. The pet market can be considered only in a minor way. Unreliable and seasonable at best, the pet market revolves around Easter, and presents a number of disadvantages. An early spring date, Easter timing requires the birth of bunnies in cold winter weather in many parts of the country. If there is one time of year a litter may not survive, this is it. Furthermore, law prevents the sale of Easter bunnies in some localities and I see (and applaud) more and more such laws being passed. What's more, the price received for Easter bunnies generally is below what you can earn in other markets. Pet stores and dealers demand large numbers of just-weaned bunnies on a specific date and for a low price. But that's only part of the problem. The rabbits often soon succumb, sometimes dying at the hands of young children who don't know when to stop squeezing or that baby bunnies can't eat lettuce or cabbage without dropping dead from diarrhea. In addition, the sale of pet rabbits hurts their image as food. Who wants to eat his pet? Rabbit meat consumption rates remain low where pet sales are high.

THE MEAT MARKET

More rabbits are raised year-round for meat than for any other use. You may sell your rabbits live to a processor, or butcher them for direct sale to the consumer. Live sales are the simplest because commercial, wholesale and retail butchering is a complex operation governed by local laws that require standards of sanitation, refrigeration, ventilation, etc., that you may be unable to meet. Home butchering is simple, however. Before you choose a breed to sell live to a processor, confer with him. He may recommend one he prefers. Because he will be buying the young rabbits you produce, you will do well to take his advice. He probably will tell you he requires rabbits of a certain weight. You will want to produce them in that weight range and will need a breed which can do the job.

NEW ZEALAND WHITES — NUMBER ONE

Americans raise more New Zealand Whites for meat than any other breed. Next in line is the Californian, followed, not necessarily in this order, by Satins, Champagne D'Argents, Chinchillas, New Zealand Reds and Blacks and Palominos. Actually, other breeds taste just as good, but several other considerations send some breeds ahead of the rest.

New Zealands and Californians wear white pelts. Many processors sell the pelts from the live rabbits, and they like white most of all. White pelts have gained this popularity because they can be dyed any color. Most rabbit fur produced in this country is used either white or dyed, sometimes in imitation of a more valuable fur.

Three champion New Zealand Whites.

CONSISTENT EXCELLENCE

What is more important, however, is that New Zealand Whites and Californians have been bred by commercial producers to a higher degree of consistent excellence than any other breed. To the breeder, this means that he can count on superior feed conversion, disease resistance, fertility, litter size and otherwise better performance compared to other breeds. To the processor, New Zealands and Californians mean white pelts, but also fine bones and good dressout - in other words, a high percentage of salable meat.

THE LABORATORY MARKET

Another market comes into play here. Some breeders and some processors sell laboratory rabbits as well as meat. New Zealands, in particular, are the choice of laboratories. Labs like them because, primarily, they can be obtained in sufficient consistent quantity to make their studies accurate. If you are buying lab rabbits, you know New Zealands are good and are available everywhere, any time.

Let's suppose you are considering the large-scale production of meat rabbits for sale live to a processor. I would say choose New Zealand Whites or Californians. Let's say you are going to sell laboratory stock as well. Then stick to New Zealand Whites unless you have a commitment from a lab for another breed. What I am trying to stress here is not to choose a breed that you are fond of, or think is cute, but one that someone who represents a market wants to buy.

LOTS AND LOTS OF RABBITS

But to make a decent profit on live meat rabbit sales to a processor requires a large volume of sales. You need to raise lots of rabbits and sell lots of rabbits. And unless you plan to produce a lot of them, it's not really worth it to concentrate solely on the production of meat or laboratory stock.

For example, meat rabbits recently brought 50 cents a pound live weight in my area. A four-pound fryer fetched $2, which may sound pretty good on the face of it. But figuring the cost of feed which was nine cents a pound, and a top feed/meat conversion ratio of 4:1 —

that is, four pounds to feed to one pound of meat — it doesn't look that good. The four-pound fryer dresses out at about 50 per cent, or two pounds. The 4:1 feed/meat conversion ratio dictates a consumption of 16 pounds of feed at a cost of $1.44, leaving 66 cents. Remember that it takes three months — from conception to market — to get that 66 cents and you can see that it will take a lot of these fryers to make you any money. Mind you now, we are merely talking about feed costs. We haven't yet considered the cost of stock, equipment and any other investments you might have in your rabbit enterprise. True, these costs are in the category of long-term investment. But how long do you want to take to recover this cash?

LAB RETURN MAY BE BETTER

At the same time, laboratory rabbits sold at $1 per pound live weight to a middleman, who picked them up at the rabbitry and resold them to a lab. This meant a return of $2.56 over the feed cost — which is a lot better. But not all your production, under the best market conditions, can be sold to laboratories. Often the order is for all one sex, perhaps females. Also, some labs want rabbits older than four-pound fryers. After four pounds, the feed conversion ratio deteriorates. So, the return of a lab/meat operation may be only about half way between that of lab and meat prices paid, minus the feed cost. You still will need a lot of rabbits to make this kind of rabbitry pay. If you can have a big rabbitry, are a good manager and enjoy a steady market, you can make money on this type of rabbitry. This will take you quite a long time, however, because no matter what kind of rabbitry you have, you must start fairly small to start right. A bonus in the future might be your own direct lab contract with a higher return than a middleman offers — but you will have to wait until you are able to be a steady enough supplier to handle it. If this kind of rabbitry appeals to you, I strongly urge you to begin it with New Zealand Whites or Californians — perhaps both. If you choose one or both of these breeds and favorable market conditions prevail, you will be on your way to a successful commercial rabbitry.

THREE WAYS TO SUCCEED

Sales of meat and laboratory stock, supplemented by breeding stock sales, are the three best ways I know to succeed with a larger rabbitry. But it takes considerable time to reach the size sufficient to make it a success, because it requires the largest investment of time and money. It may take all your spare time unless you have help — and you may build it into a full-time business. Of course, it also will take the proximity of a processor and a lab — both of which will largely control the price you receive — to take your output.

MEAT ON YOUR OWN TABLE

Suppose your intent is merely to raise rabbits for your own table. You still can't go wrong with New Zealand Whites or Californians, and at current feed prices you can put meat on your table for 72 cents a pound. If you sell some to a processor or a lab, you can have your rabbit dinner for free!

But now you have many additional breeds to choose from. You don't have to meet rigid production schedules or worry whether the processor will pay you less for rabbits wearing colored pelts. In fact, you might choose a rabbit of a particular color or pattern and save the pelts for craft projects of your own choosing, even a fur coat. You don't even have to raise a particular size of rabbit.

DON'T OVERLOOK THE SMALL BREEDS

For the past several years I have raised smaller breeds and can tell you that they taste just as good. As a matter of fact, I'm convinced that, all things considered, the meat of the smaller breeds can be produced more economically per pound, if you don't count the labor involved. The problem lies in finding a productive strain of small rabbits. True too, is the fact that few processors want a smaller rabbit because of the extra time it takes to process the same amount of meat a larger rabbit offers. My favorite breed is the Tan, which weighs about five or six pounds at maturity, about the same as the Dutch, a breed I used to raise. Tans don't produce New Zealand-size litters consistently, but eat half what the big whites do and need less space. Furthermore, they have finer bones and a faster early growth, producing a more finished carcass at a younger age.

The small Tans require little feed or space.

HOW SMALL BREEDS DRESS OUT

While Tans never reach four pounds in eight weeks, they will weigh three pounds in that time. I often dress them out at 10 to 12 weeks, when they weigh 3¼ to 3½ pounds, delivering about as much meat as an eight-week New Zealand because there is less waste.

I don't suggest you raise Dwarfs or Polish for meat, because you would get little more than a pound from a mature animal. I'd remind you, though, that the woods still are full of hunters who seek an even smaller animal and fill their pots with several to make Brunswick Stew — from squirrels.

The main thing to remember when it comes to raising meat rabbits is that when you plan to sell them live, you must meet the buyer's demands. But if you plan to eat them yourself, or can develop your own customers for fresh or frozen meat, you may select almost any breed you like. And for the small family, this might mean, as it does for me, a small breed.

As for the prospects of the small, backyard breeder such as myself, I'm sold on the concept of the small breeds. If you can have only a few rabbits, it seems to me the smaller breeds make a lot of sense.

THE BREEDING STOCK MARKET

Profit on a meat or laboratory operation, we have seen, comes only with large volume. A small raiser then, in my opinion, should concentrate on sales of breeding stock to prospective meat and lab stock producers and fanciers, sell only occasionally to the meat and lab markets, and then only if there are enough left after consigning the culls to your own freezer.

I'm a backyard breeder with only 36 hutches in a 10 foot by 20 foot building. I really have neither time nor space for anything larger. I just couldn't handle it without giving it more time, which I am reluctant to do, or more space, of which there is none. After years of raising other breeds, I chose the small breed of Tan for a number of reasons that make sense to me. First, the Tan is a very fancy breed which challenges the breeder when it comes to producing top specimens. Body markings and color are important considerations. Therefore, sales of these rabbits to other breeders bring a high unit price. My current price for young stock is about $15 each. Because these rabbits consume half what the larger ones do, it costs me far less than a dollar to raise this $15 rabbit. In addition, the cages are only about half the size of those for larger stock, so the cost to house them is reduced along with the feed. Also, I can house twice as many Tans in the same space I'd need for larger rabbits. And I can even raise them faster, because they mature earlier and reproduce sooner than larger rabbits.

YOU HAVE TO ADVERTISE

There is a hitch of course. I have to spend money to advertise, and because Tans primarily are show rabbits, I have to exhibit them regularly and win often. Showing costs little but does take time — usually on Sundays in the spring and fall months. For me this is an enjoyable activity, mostly because I enjoy the company of other rabbit breeders, but certainly also because of the fun of the competition and the tips to be gained from other breeders and the rabbit judges. And there's no denying the thrill you get when you win. Shows also make a fine family outing.

ECONOMICS OF A SMALL RABBITRY

But consider the economics of a small rabbitry where individuals sell for $20 compared to $2 or $4, including even the costs of advertising (not too high, really — some is free!) and the sales effort that must be made. The potential per unit of space simply is much greater for the small producer of breeding stock — and, I think, even greater for the small producer of *small* breeding stock. Because not all the production is up to breeding stock standards, there still are rabbits for the freezer, or the processor, or for your own customers, and pelts for sale or for your own use.

After having run this kind of rabbitry for several years, I'm now at the point where half of my 36 hutches contain breeding does. The rest are for bucks and young growing stock. This rabbitry produced about 350 youngsters last year. About 275 were sold for breeding stock — the rest went for meat one way or another. None was sold for Easter pets, I might add, although a few did become pets of local youngsters, and I gave a few away. Most of the breeding stock was sold as the result of magazine advertising and was shipped by air express to almost every state in the union and to some locations beyond our boundaries. Some were sold at the 10 shows I attended and a few were sold locally. Actually, I could sell more locally if I wanted to, but I prefer mail order sales as a way of doing business. In any case, it can be seen that the return on my small rabbitry is much greater than it would be if I tried to produce meat and laboratory stock. I should add that because I have a small rabbitry I have more time for other pursuits. These include the custom manufacture of rabbit hutches which brings the rabbitry additional funds each year. Of course, I have a full-time job — one that occasionally requires extra hours and considerable travel — a situation that actually dictates a small rabbitry. My older son is a reliable backstop when I can't be at home. I also have a lot of other interests, ranging from gardening and cabinet-making to trout fishing and Little League and Boy Scout work. Rabbits are only part of the picture.

YOU HAVE TO FIND THE CUSTOMER

You might wonder about the extent of the breeding stock market. Initially, you will purchase a pair or more of rabbits from a breeder who sells breeding stock. Regardless of your market, you need to start with breeding stock. Breeding stock is thus a market in itself but it requires a customer who wants to raise rabbits and there are fewer of these than customers who want to eat rabbits. Nevertheless, breeding stock is a promising market because the number of persons who want to raise rabbits is increasing and their markets are expanding.

I mentioned already that membership in the American Rabbit Breeders Association more than doubled recently. These and many other thousands of people all became customers for breeding stock. As this is written, breeding stock demand continues to be brisk, and the outlook for continued growth is great because more and more Americans are awakening to the possible rewards of raising rabbits.

If you raise really fine rabbits and are willing to make the effort required, you will always be able to sell breeding stock. If you start right, by starting with good stock, you will be able to sell breeding stock immediately. And what you sell will be just as good as what you bought — perhaps better.

CHOOSE ALMOST ANY BREED

The breeding stock market is wide open when it comes to a choice of breeds. I have already stated a case for the small, fancy breeds but potential breeders seeking stock may be interested in either or all of the three major markets themselves, and just about any breed will serve you well, from the most popular to the most obscure.

There really are two ways to look at the breeding stock market: Select either a breed that is popular and in great demand, such as the New Zealand White, or one that is largely unavailable except from you — perhaps the Harlequin. In fact, a combination of these two may serve you well. I raised Dutch, a perennially popular small breed, for several years, while also raising Tans, then a little known variety, to give two strings to my bow. While I worked to promote Tans, the Dutch supported the effort. Once the Tans began to gain acceptance, I was able to discard the Dutch. Today only Tans reside in my rabbitry and I find myself the president of the American Tan Rabbit Specialty Club and editor of the club newsletter, with a steady demand for my stock.

While the choice of a breed is pretty much up to you when it comes to breeding stock, one consideration is paramount. You must have purebred rabbits. And while purebred stock is not a necessity for some other purposes, starting right dictates, to my mind, only the best available. And these are, almost without exception, purebred rabbits.

3
The Right
Foundation Stock

Better than anything else, purebred stock will help you start raising rabbits the modern way, no matter why you raise them.

Purebred rabbits are pedigreed. Pedigreed rabbits may or may not be registered, and registered rabbits may or may not be worth buying, but nevertheless will be important to you.

These terms — purebred, pedigreed, registered and others — can be confusing. Let's untangle them and discuss their relative significance. But first, let's mention the crossbreds.

LOWEST ON THE TOTEM POLE — CROSSBREDS

Crossbred rabbits are mongrels. They are of mixed ancestry, perhaps of the Heinz 57 variety, or perhaps very close to purebred. They might even in fact be purebred, but have no pedigree paper to prove it and thus must be considered crossbred.

Crossbred rabbits carry the least value of any. Nobody really knows what ancestors went before them, and nobody really knows what progeny will descend from them. I have seen all kinds of crossbreds, and I wouldn't consider owning any of them. I never have. You can't predict what they will do for you, other than eat as much or more as the best rabbits while returning to you the least. Nobody wants crossbreds; not even the meat processor, although he will probably take them. He doesn't have much idea how they will dress out; whether they will give him lots of meat or lots of bone.

You don't know how much they will cost to feed, how readily they will breed, how prolifically they will produce, how hardily they will resist disease, or anything else much about them. If you like surprises, crossbreds are for you. If you want profitable, healthy, thrifty, handsome rabbits, forget about them. An ironic fact about crossbreds is that the 4-H kids in my locale who insist upon keeping crossbreds enter them in their shows in a class they call "commercial," and they call the crossbreds "commercials." The fact is, these commercials have less commercial value than any others, particularly those noncommercials, the purebreds.

A PEDIGREED RABBIT HAS "PAPERS"

A purebred rabbit is bred to a certain written physical description, called a standard. Purebreds are also called standardbred or thoroughbred and these terms are nearly synonymous with another used to describe them — pedigreed. This purebred rabbit has a written record of its ancestry — a pedigree — as evidence of its pure breeding.

A typical pedigree is illustrated. This pedigree is the "paper" you should get with your pedigreed rabbit. Note that the pedigree shown contains the names and other information about three generations of ancestors on both sides of the family. This includes private ear identification numbers, registration numbers if registered, color, weight, winnings and perhaps a note or two about the size of the litter in which it was born or how it ranked in the litter relative to the others in the opinion of the breeder. The more information, the better to determine the rabbit's ultimate value as a breeder.

NO PAPER — NOT PEDIGREED

Remember this about pedigreed rabbits: If you don't get the pedigree paper, the rabbit is not, for all practical purposes, pedigreed,

A.R.B.A. Rabbit Pedigree

no matter how purebred it actually may be, because you can't prove it. Without the paper, the rabbit is worth considerably less as a breeder. If you are wise, you will take no rabbits without pedigree papers.

REGISTRATION

A pedigreed rabbit may also be a registered rabbit, but the two terms are not synonymous, although it would appear that many newcomers to rabbit raising think so. A registered rabbit must be purebred, have a pedigree paper and be a mature specimen. It must then be examined by a licensed American Rabbit Breeders Association registrar. He must certify it to be free of apparent physical defects. In the registrar's opinion, it must meet the minimum physical requirements of the breed as described in the written breed standard. It should, for example, be of the correct size and weight, color and body type, among other considerations. And the registrar has to examine the rabbit and certify, signing his name to an affidavit, that the rabbit passes his inspection. He puts his reputation on the line — and his right to the registrar license — every time he signs. Remember, there is none of the American Kennel Club sort of thing where you simply send in the papers of the sire and dam and your litter of puppies gains registration. A personal examination is required. This procedure makes rabbit registration just about the best animal registry system there is.

Rabbit Registration

Certificate of Entry in the Stud Book of

AMERICAN RABBIT BREEDERS ASSOCIATION, INCORPORATED   No. 1573 G

NAME Sweet Son   EAR NO. BB6D   BREED Tan   SEX Buck   COLOR Chocolate

BORN 7-25-72   WEIGHT 4½   WINNINGS 1st Jr. Buck (8), B.O.S. (50) BOSV (5) Monteo   DATE 11-23-73
RBA 1973, Fairfield Co. RBA 1973, Green Mt. RBA 1973

NAME OF BREEDER Robert Bennett   ADDRESS 624 Lawlins Road Wyckoff, N. J.

PURCHASED FROM

REGISTRAR'S NAME Charles Lyons   ADDRESS Rutland, Vermont

DESCRIPTION/TYPE Very good (compact)   BONE Medium   COLOR Very Good   BODY Very Good   FUR Good fly-back & texture

HEAD Full   EARS Length 3½"   EYES Clear   CONDITION Very Good   BALANCE Good

REMARKS Very nice chocolate tan, very good markings.

OWNER Robert Bennett   STREET 624 Lawlins Road   TOWN Wyckoff   STATE New Jersey

DATE FILED 12-5-73

SIRE Sir Brian   REG. NO. 424G   WT. 4½
COLOR Lilac

SIRE English Import   REG. NO.
COLOR K.B. 70 Lilac   WT. 5

In England

In England

Buckeye Lad   WT. 5
COLOR Lilac

SIRE Harriet   REG. NO. 433C   WT. 4½
COLOR Chocolate

Princess of Kirklees   REG. NO. 1267B   WT. 5½
COLOR Chocolate

DAM Bittersweet   REG. NO. 3997B   WT. 4½
COLOR Chocolate

SIRE Shera' Man   WT. 4½
COLOR Chocolate

Sir Ralph   REG. NO. 2027B   WT. 4½
COLOR Chocolate

Mary L.   WT. 4½
COLOR Chocolate

DAM Deck-Me-Jo   WT. 4
COLOR Chocolate

Sir Ralph   REG. NO. 2027B   WT. 4½
COLOR Chocolate

Lady Clara   REG. NO. 974G   WT. 5½
COLOR Chocolate

Secretary

Only members of the American Rabbit Breeders Association may apply for registration of their stock, but anyone may, of course, be the owner of such animals. The fee is $2 per rabbit, which is paid to the registrar. His remuneration actually is only $1, because the other $1 goes to the ARBA, which files a copy of the registration certificate at its headquarters registry, and issues a certificate to the owner of the rabbit. Such a certificate is shown in the accompanying photo.

WHAT DOES IT ALL MEAN?

Now what does all this really mean to you, the new breeder? Why should you care whether the stock you start with is purebred, pedigreed and registered? Why, for instance, does it matter if rabbits you are going to raise to eat have a fancy pedigree or registration certificate behind them?

Well, not only does it matter, it actually is vital if you are to start right and be a success. That's what this book is all about, and if it could have only one chapter, this would be it.

Let's suppose you have decided to raise meat rabbits for your own table. You have calculated that the low feed cost to produce a pound of tasty meat for your family is worth the effort you will have to make to put it on the table. And you have chosen New Zealand Whites as the best breed to deliver the goods for you. So far so good.

PAPERS ARE THE PROOF

Now you go out to buy New Zealand Whites. You see a sign along a rural road, "Rabbits For Sale." The owner shows you white rabbits and says they are New Zealands. But how do you really know that's what they are? You don't unless he shows you some records of ancestry — pedigrees — to prove it. He must have kept these records and in so doing used them to maintain a herd of breeders that meets the standard for New Zealands.

Let's go back a bit and discuss further this "standard." This written physical description of the breed is prepared by members of the breed specialty club — in this case, the American Federation of New Zealand Rabbit Breeders. A "Standard Committee" of these members, composed of expert breeders, decides precisely what the New Zealand White will look like. They write this description down and the members of the Federation vote on it. If a majority agrees, the standard is submitted to the Standards Committee of the American Rabbit Breeders Association, which is the parent organization of all the breed specialty clubs. The ARBA Standards Committee, if it votes approval of the standard, admits it for publication in a volume entitled the "Standard of Perfection," which the ARBA publishes and revises every five years. This book includes the standard for every breed that the ARBA recognizes. Every breeder should own this book, or at least a copy of the standard for his chosen breed, and he should study this standard so that he will make certain he is carrying out a breeding program that will produce animals in accord with it. For example, in the case of New Zealands, if the fur should be wooly, the rabbit would be disqualified in a show and possibly would produce wooly offspring. Not only would this soon lead to a rabbitry full of disqualified rabbits, but the fur soon would be worthless. This makes a difference when you breed for show, certainly, but also if you attempt to sell breeding stock or even meat to a processor who sells the pelt. Nobody wants disqualified stock.

YOU MAY HAVE FOUND
GOOD RABBITS

If the man with the sign along the road is familiar with the standard, has breeding records of all of his stock, and provides a detailed pedigree that indicates his stock meets the required weight and color, among other things, he *probably* has good stock. If, in addition, his rabbits are also registered, you know that they have met the minimum physical requirements for the breed, and you can view the stock with great confidence. If on top of this, the pedigree and registration papers indicate show winnings, if the rabbitry is clean and the stock obviously well cared for and prolific; that is, with lots of litters on the grow, you have found a breeder from whom you certainly might buy — one who is raising rabbits the modern way.

SEVERAL ASSURANCES

For you, the prospective producer of meat for your table, there are several assurances here that you otherwise would not obtain. These white rabbits, purported to be New Zealands, will in fact reproduce their own kind, will gain weight properly, will convert feed to meat efficiently, will produce a usable or salable pelt, will be healthy if properly cared for, will be prolific and will otherwise be attractive and desired by others. They will, in fact, be worth buying. They will, in fact, start you raising rabbits the modern way.

Now you might ask if he could in fact forge all this paperwork and the answer is that he could fake some but not all, that it has been tried before, but is not likely. A pedigree is only as good as the man who writes it, to be sure. But if the man who writes it from his breeding records bothers to write it at all, the chances are excellent that he has at least kept track of what he is doing. And if he has done that, he is probably doing a pretty good job of breeding. It is the man who keeps no breeding records at all who has nothing to offer you.

THE BREEDER FROM WHOM TO BUY

With all this in mind, let's take a look at the breeder who is best qualified to sell rabbits to you — the one who will start you right.

Buy rabbits only from the very best, most highly respected breeders of your chosen breed that you can find. There probably are only a handful of these breeders for the more obscure varieties, but the United States boasts quite a number who raise the most popular breeds. There is good breeding stock to be had if you can find it, and it isn't that difficult to do.

The breeder from whom you should buy is one who, if he produces meat and laboratory stock, consistently outproduces his competitors, and gets top dollar for his production. Processors often pay him a premium; laboratories seek him out. He makes a profit from his rabbits. He makes money. He doesn't "just pay the grain." He is prosperous.

A WINNER —
WITH REGISTERED BREEDERS

If he sells show and breeding stock, he is a consistent winner. He has trophies and ribbons to show you. Lots of them. He wins year in and year out. Not the top prize every time — nobody does that. But he is up there among the winners almost every time.

In addition, he keeps his breeders registered. He provides a pedigree paper with every rabbit. He produces quite a few rabbits. Not necessarily thousands, but probably a few hundred or more every year. He is a member of ARBA. He is also a member of the breed specialty club, and probably a member of the local club. He is active in these organizations. He shows his rabbits at almost every chance he gets. His reputation, within at least his breed specialty club, is national. There are people to ask about him. Lots of people who have bought rabbits from him are happy with them.

SATISFACTION GUARANTEED

This is a breeder who stands behind every rabbit he sells. He tells you that he guarantees your complete satisfaction, that he will refund your money or exchange your rabbits for others for any reason, even a stupid one. His reason is simply that above all considerations he raises rabbits because of the satisfaction he derives from them, and if you aren't happy he isn't either.

His rabbitry is neat and clean. His rabbits are perfectly clean and healthy. And he is delighted to show them to you. He wants you to see the fine conditions under which they are kept. And he won't let *you* pick out the rabbits, at least not on sight alone.

HOW TO FIND HIM

How will you find the rabbitry that will supply you with your foundation stock? Probably not by a sign along the road. Follow this procedure and you can't go wrong: First, decide upon a breed. Follow my recommendations in Chapter 2. If you haven't yet made up your mind, attend a nearby rabbit show where nearly all kinds will be on display. Look them all over. You can find the date and location of the nearest upcoming show in *Domestic Rabbits* magazine. This magazine, which you will receive if you are a member of the American Rabbit Breeders Association, lists upcoming shows in each issue. Write or phone the listed show secretary if you need directions to the show. Make sure you see all the different breeds you possibly can find, because you will be much happier in your choice and less likely to change to another breed in short order.

When you decide on a breed, watch it being judged, and talk to the breeders. Ask where they got their breeding stock — who they recommend. Perhaps they will have some stock for sale themselves, but don't buy any at the show. It's a poor idea to buy rabbits in a showroom, especially if you buy them because they are winners. Don't buy a rabbit based on its performance on the show table one day, although you may buy rabbits at a show if they are brought there especially for you.

RESIST THE TEMPTATION TO BUY AT A SHOW

I see many persons purchasing rabbits at shows, and sometimes sell them there myself, although I really don't think too much of the idea for beginners. It's all right for the experienced breeder, who perhaps adds a buck or doe to his herd in an effort to improve certain characteristics or simply to infuse new blood into his line, but it's not a good idea for the beginner. So go take a look at the rabbits at the show, but don't plan to buy any. You might become interested in those of a certain breeder, and, if so, obtain an invitation to visit his rabbitry. If his rabbitry meets the standards just covered, he may be a good man from whom to buy.

It is possible, however, that you will not find an expert breeder of your chosen breed at the show. Or, if you do, he may not have sufficient stock to sell you. Do not despair, however, because your best chance to get good stock is now beckoning.

MAIL ORDER CAN BE THE ANSWER

This is the time to consider purchasing by mail. If you observe the classified pages of *Domestic Rabbits,* and *Rabbits* magazine, you will discover the names of breeders who have stock for sale. These breeders can supply stock to newcomers and oldtimers alike all over the nation, and their rabbits are so respected that they are bought sight unseen.

You should, however, before sending off any letters, determine who has the best stock to sell. One way to do this is to join the breed specialty club of your chosen breed and read the club newsletter. In the newsletter you will find show reports and sweepstakes point standings, and it is from among the winners of these shows and leaders of these standings that you will want to consider making your purchase. If these breeders are among those advertising stock for sale in *Domestic Rabbits* or in the club newsletter, write and tell them what you propose to do. You can do this with great confidence that your letters will be well received and that you are on your way to obtaining good stock, because you are writing to a breeder who is among the best in the nation.

HE STARTED RIGHT

First of all, he started with the best possible stock himself. Then he improved it over a long period of time. He has shown and won consistently, and he breeds quite a number of rabbits, but sells only the best as breeding stock. A good number go for meat or to labs, even if he has been at it for some time, because his standards are so high and get higher year after year. The rabbits he would have sold or kept as breeders last year will not measure up to this year's output, because he has worked hard to upgrade his herd through selective breeding. This is, for him, a never-ending process. He buys advertising, for which he pays with part of the money he receives from breeding stock sales. He charges a good price, so he can afford the ads. And he advertises so he will be able to breed large numbers of rabbits continually, and thus stay ahead of the other breeders. All this is precisely why he has the best rabbits of this breed that you can find.

He will sell you good stock, and he will stand behind it. He will guarantee these rabbits will do well for you if you do right by them. He will answer all your questions in the mail, and be interested in your success, which of course is an extension of his own. He has a vested interest in you. He wants you to make good with his stock. Later on he may read the show reports in the same newsletter you first read about him, and find that you are now up among the winners in your area shows. He will derive a lot of satisfaction and his chief reward from this, you can be sure.

WHAT TO EXPECT

Now what should you expect to be able to buy? You should not expect to buy his best breeders. He won't sell them. But you should expect young stock out of his best, or possibly some of his older breeders that he would like to move out to make room for youngsters.

Your best bet would be to ask him to provide you with some of his best young stock and perhaps also some of his best older stock, depending on how fast you wish to get going. Do not expect to get his grand champions, unless you want them more than he does and are willing to prove it with your pocketbook. Do not even expect to buy show winners, although the young stock you purchase may in fact go on to win great titles. Buying a show winner proves only, in most cases, that you can spend a lot of money. Producing your own show winner is light years more satisfying. It is fair to add, however, that some breeders produce so many winners at so many shows that they do have winners for sale at reasonable prices. If such is the case, do not hesitate to take them.

French Lop is one of special breeds new to U.S.

FOUR IS A GOOD NUMBER

Ask any successful breeder how to start your rabbitry and he probably will tell you: *small*. Even if you plan a large rabbitry, don't expect to purchase all of the herd of breeders you expect ultimately to own.

A good start includes a minimum of four rabbits. I wouldn't try to build a herd from a single pair, or even a trio of two does and a buck, which is a popular way to start. A couple of junior bucks, a junior doe and a bred senior doe make an ideal start.

If you ask for two junior bucks and a junior doe, you should expect to get them from the very best of the top breeders in the herd. The senior doe perhaps will be as much as two years old and have only a year or so of breeding life left. Nevertheless, if this doe has been producing in a good rabbitry for 18 months already, she must be pretty good. Otherwise she would not have hung around so long. Ask to have her bred to the best buck the breeder recommends. If she produces a litter, the next time she is due for mating one of the junior bucks will be ready to use. Also, the other junior pair will be ready for mating. So, in about three or four months, you could have your original four rabbits, a litter of youngsters and two more litters on the way.

Now why do I suggest two bucks and two does? Well, you probably will always want to keep open the option of selling some breeding stock yourself, no matter why you raise rabbits, and you want to start yourself with a fairly broad base for further breeding. With two bucks and two does, you will be able to sell and breed from pairs and trios from two different litters from four different parents. And such off-spring are usually more desirable than, for example, a brother-sister pair. I will go into the rationale behind this notion in Chapter 6, but for now keep in mind that two pairs are the minimum.

HOW TO BUILD YOUR HERD

Let's suppose you take my recommendation and purchase four rabbits in January. The senior doe kindles a litter in February and you decide to save the best three does and the best buck from this litter. Later on, in May, the junior doe kindles and so does the senior doe again. You save the best three does from each of these litters, and the best buck from each. By summer, you have bred the original senior doe again, the original junior doe, and the three does from the first litter. You have five litters on the way, but you also have six junior does to breed in the fall, and a choice of four eager young bucks with which to mate them. Before winter you will have 11 breeding does, more juniors growing, a fine selection of stud bucks, and litters all over the place. Your four original rabbits are now 100, and you have saved only the best.

Maybe you don't want 100, and maybe you won't get quite that many, but it could happen if you want it to. And all this time you will be learning their habits, which is something you should attempt only on a limited scale, because there is a surprising amount to be learned. It is a simple matter to calculate just how fast you want to start, from the above example, and of course there is the necessity of providing housing for all the rabbits you will produce, so that again will have a bearing on your start. You need not, of course, save as many young does as I'm suggesting here. If you do not want so many rabbits, by all means save only the very best one from each litter and, in fact, replace one of your original does with a better one should it come along. But please do not make a smaller start than with four rabbits if you have the slightest intention of selling any breeding stock or of building yourself even the most limited herd.

PAY A FAIR PRICE

So explain in your letter that you would like to purchase two bucks and two does as discussed above. Tell him you are willing to rely on his judgment in selection of these rabbits because he will know best which ones will go together to make you a good start. Be prepared to pay the price he asks, and remember that you get what you pay for. Don't shell out a lot of money for rabbits with fancy show records unless you are rich and foolish, but be willing to pay a decent price for good stock. These prices probably will be at least $10 each, but more likely in the $20 range for juniors and $30 to $40 or even more for seniors.

RELY ON HIS JUDGMENT

Don't insist upon "unrelated" rabbits, but depend upon his judgment as to which pairs to send. In Chapter 6, I'll cover various methods of breeding, but for now let me say that more often than not, unrelated rabbits will not do the job nearly as well as related stock. The main thing to do is to pick a breeder of good reputation and put your trust in him. This is true even if you purchase your rabbits in person at his rabbitry. Have the breeder select your stock for you. Nobody knows his stock as he does. And nobody knows which animal will go best with another better than he does.

SENDING IN YOUR ORDER

It is a simple matter to order. First, have your hutches ready. Then send the breeder a check or money order for the rabbits, along with a letter giving your complete name, mailing address and phone number. He will let you know a mutually agreeable shipping date and you will be phoned by the local air express office at the airport nearest you to pick up your rabbits. You drive down there and get them and pay the shipping charges, which will vary depending on the number and weight of the rabbits. For four rabbits, to almost any place in the United States, the cost will be no more than $25, and probably a lot less. You can have them delivered directly to your door, but this takes more time, perhaps an extra day, and can cost you another $5 or $10.

The shipper can get them to you the same day if he ships from a major airport and if you receive them at a major airport. If both of you live in Podunk, it could take two or three days. Fear not for the comfort of your rabbits, for they are hardy travelers. In my own case, living near Burlington, Vermont, I am able to get rabbits to rabbitries all over the country the same day I ship, about the same time it takes rabbits to travel to a show and home. This helps get them there in good condition. In fact, to my knowledge, only one rabbit of the many hundreds I have shipped ever has expired en route. And of course, the express company made good on it because I insured the shipment. Everything else being equal, if you can find a shipper who ships from a major airport, your chances of a successful trip for your rabbits will increase.

THEY NEED PEACE AND QUIET

When you get them home, install them in their hutches with food and drink and then let them alone. They need a little time to get used to their surroundings. Then write or phone the shipper and let him know you have them and that they are okay and that you are, in fact, a little thrilled with them. Then he will send you the pedigree papers, each one marked with a number that corresponds with a number in the rabbit's ear. He should also send you the date your senior doe was bred and the pedigree paper of the buck to which she was mated.

THE BEST EAT NO MORE THAN THE WORST

You say you want rabbits only for your own table, so why bother to invest in the best? Again I say it costs no more to feed and house the best rabbits, and that your potential is much greater, even for producing meat for your own table consistently, if you start with the best breeding stock available. Also, you will take a lot of pride in good rabbits; none in bad. Furthermore, they will be admired and sought by others and you will find a demand for them. Keep ever in mind that you will always, if you are a success, produce more rabbits than you will be able to use yourself. Good as they are, nobody wants to eat rabbit every day.

WATCH OUT FOR "BUY-BACKS"

Now that I've told you from whom to buy rabbits, I'm going to tell you especially from whom not to buy. Don't buy them from the so-called buy-back concerns. You may have seen their ads. They go something like this:

"Raise Rabbits For Us. $30,000 a Year in Your Backyard! Big Profits Await You!"

Avoid these firms, which usually advertise in outdoor and mechanical hobby magazines, and forget about getting rich quick raising rabbits. You will not get rich quick. You will get poor quick.

Here's the way these firms operate. They offer to sell you breeding stock at fairly high prices (*extremely* high for what you get). Then they tell you that they will buy (sometimes they promise, sometimes they don't) the offspring back from you at a lower price, but one that doesn't seem too bad.

HERE'S HOW YOU LOSE

But here's the hitch: You have to pay the shipping charges, and these costs eat up all or so much of the profit that you really can't afford to sell and they really don't have to buy. They may even insist that you sell all your youngsters to them or else the whole deal is off. This means that in order to build your herd you can't save youngsters for future breeders, but will have to purchase all your breeding stock from them. You can see how much more expensive this can be.

But if there's still a worse aspect to all this, here it is. They really don't even send you the rabbits you order and in fact may not even own any at all, or just a few. Your rabbits come from someone else who bought from them, and you get whatever that someone wants to get rid of, which usually is the worst he has because he is getting so little for them (only a fraction of what you paid; only the amount they promise to pay you). You order from the buy-back and you become just another mean little link in a miserable chain. The buy-backs have probably done more to hinder rabbit raising than any other single factor.

WHAT A SURPRISE I GOT

I remember visiting one such establishment a few years ago. I was driving in the area of this buy-back, and had received some of its promotional pamphlets. I thought I would stop in at this big rabbit farm and have a look at a few thousand of their best animals. I couldn't really believe I was at the right address when I knocked at the owner's door and this rather cranky man complained that I hadn't called or written for an appointment. The thought had never occurred to me that such a private, individual arrangement would be necessary for a visit to a nationally known rabbit farm. Well, as long as I was there, he'd sign me up for a few rabbits, and invited me in. It was, of course, out, that I wanted to go, out to his rabbitry, out to see all the rabbits. He didn't really want to show them to me, but finally took me out in the back of his house to present six rabbits in some dilapidated hutches — six of the most ordinary and unspectacular rabbits I had ever seen. This was, he quickly explained, merely the sales headquarters. All the great rabbits were spread out over the country in the backyards of America. The orders came in from the national advertising and he sent them out to his "cooperating breeders." And these are the people who filled them. He never saw the rabbits he sold, never determined whether they were healthy. And he only cared if he got a complaint.

ARBA ISSUES WARNINGS

You will never find ads of buy-backs in *Domestic Rabbits* magazine, because the American Rabbit Breeders Association won't let them in. ARBA warns its members continually about these firms. This should be caution enough for you. If the nation's largest organization dedicated to rabbit raising says to avoid these outfits, it would seem that they should be avoided. So far it appears that these concerns are not illegal, only unethical. So they stay in business (or, as one did last year, go bankrupt while owing several hundred thousand dollars to hundreds of people who ordered rabbits and who never got any, not even inferior ones). But you shouldn't help keep them in business. Not if you want to raise rabbits the modern way.

4
Housing
And Equipment

Next to the right foundation breeding stock, the right housing and equipment will do the most to insure your success with rabbits.

The environment you provide for your stock affects their health, growth and productivity to be sure, but it can even be the difference between raising rabbits or not at all. Wherever zoning laws prohibit this activity, rabbit housing lies behind the prohibition. And wherever there is distaste for rabbit raising it is based on the looks of a rabbitry and on housing that produces bad smells, rodents and flies. The wrong housing can stop you from having rabbits altogether, or if you have them, it can make them unhealthy, unproductive and a stinking eyesore.

Too often a prospective rabbit raiser looks at some old wooden hutches of a current raiser, obtains lumber and chicken wire, hammer and nails and begins to build a similar structure. And too often the results are disastrous. A wooden hutch absolutely will not do. There is only one kind of hutch worth using, whether you build it yourself (and you can, as you soon will see) or buy it. That is the all-wire hutch. Compared to any other kind of hutch you can build or buy, the all-wire hutch is a winner. There is no way any other kind of hutch can touch it. I urge you to consider no other kind.

If you use it outdoors, it will need some protection from the weather, depending upon your climate, but indoors it is fine the way it is. If it is possible to locate your hutch within a building of some sort, you will be providing this protection in a single unit. If you need to protect your hutches singly or in small multiples you will find it a simple matter with the all-wire hutch.

Consider first of all what kind of living quarters a rabbit requires. He needs clean quarters. He needs plenty of light and ventilation. He needs protection from winds and drafts, but can take plenty of cold. He cannot stand extreme heat. He needs a dry hutch, all the way around. He can't have a leaky roof and he can't stand a wet floor or a damp atmosphere. He does not need a lot of room. Domestic rabbits are not used to hopping great distances as are their wild cousins. But they do need enough room to rear a family comfortably without over-crowding.

Next, consider what kind of a hutch you, the rabbit keeper, need. The hutch must prevent escape. It must be easy to clean; self-cleaning if possible. It must be easy to handle, adaptable to inside or outside use (you may start out with outside hutches and later move them into a shed). It must be durable. It must allow you to feed and water the rabbits conveniently, without even opening the door, if possible. It must allow you to see what is going on inside at all times, because it is the observant rabbit keeper whose stock thrives. It must allow you to catch and handle the rabbits with ease. And it must be inexpensive and easy to build or buy.

THE ALL-WIRE HUTCH

Enter the all-wire hutch. This is the most advanced hutch in use today, and it is the easiest and most economical to build or buy. You can see from the photo that the hutch is self-cleaning. Only an occasional wire-brushing is needed, plus periodic disinfecting, which is easy to accomplish. Droppings and urine fall right through to the ground or to pans. Complete ventilation is afforded. Feeders steal none of the hutch floor space. Feeders can be filled from outside, and the most modern, labor-saving devices for water can be used, or crocks can be filled without opening the hutch. This saves time in proportion to the number of rabbits you have. The hutch will last for many years, because the rabbit will not be able to gnaw it. And years from now, unlike wooden hutches which will be soaked with urine and gnawed to pieces, your wire hutch will still be serviceable and doubtless worth more money than it cost. This is a fact. I built some of these hutches just a few years ago for about half what they cost to build today. And yet today, as then, they cost less to build than any other kind.

Efficient home-built cages hung from assembled iron framework.

Why don't more rabbit raisers use the all-wire hutch? Well, more and more are doing so, and commercial raisers use nothing else. But too many hobbyists and other small raisers simply are not aware of their existence or think they might be expensive or difficult to build, or because they are more familiar with woodworking tools and shy away from working with metal. And then, there are those who harbor misconceptions about the needs of a rabbit. They think he needs cozier quarters and that wood will provide them. They forget that the fur-bearing rabbit will grow a thicker coat to ward off the winter chill. Some honestly believe the wire floor will hurt the rabbits' feet. They forget about old Thumper in Felix Salton's book *Bambi.* Thumper was the rabbit who periodically stomped a thickly padded hind foot (which rabbit raisers call the hock). Like Thumper, the domestic rabbit has very big furry feet and can take it.

HOW TO MAKE A WIRE HUTCH

Here's how to make the wire hutch. You can build your first one just as well as I build mine. I have put together many hundreds of them and can complete one in less than half an hour. But your first attempt will probably take a couple of hours. You won't make a mess of sawdust, nor will there be any loud banging or sawing. I build them in the basement in cold weather, in the garage when it's nice. You will need only pliers and wire cutters, and your cost will be less than if you used lumber and screws and hinges and assorted hardware.

For the front, back and sides, purchase in a hardware, farm supply or department store a length of one-inch by two-inch welded 14-gauge galvanized wire fencing (sometimes called turkey wire). It should be 18 inches wide, so the hutch will be high enough to let the rabbits stretch up on their hind legs. For a cage with a floor area of 2½ by 3 feet, fine for all but the giant breeds, which need an extra foot or two, you will need an 11-foot piece.

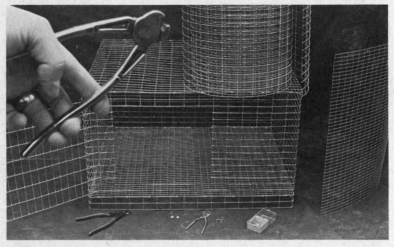

Cage is made with finer 1 x ½ mesh for the floor.

Don't cut this wire, but lay it flat on the floor and bend four corners by hammering it around a length of 2x4 lumber. Don't bend against the welds. Fasten it into a rectangle using hog rings, which can be purchased in auto supply stores, strangely enough, because they are used to fasten auto seat covers, not hogs. They come with a special pair of pliers and usually cost a dollar or less including the pliers. You may do without these rings if you twist the cut ends of the wire with pliers. Or, you may purchase very inexpensively C-rings or J-clips from suppliers of rabbitry equipment. These rings and clips may be bought by the pound and you can get enough for a hutch with only change. If you use these rings or clips, clamp them on the wire with pliers about every three inches or so. You've now got all four sides of the hutch assembled.

For the floor, buy a length of half-inch by one-inch mesh, 16 gauge or 14 gauge (the latter is heavier and better, but initially more expensive) welded, galvanized wire (not hardware cloth — it doesn't have the necessary rigidity). For your 2½ by 3 foot hutch, you'll need a piece 30 by 36 inches. Fasten this to the bottom, using rings or clips or by twisting short pieces of wire around the sections. The top will be the same size and go on the same way, but use the one-inch by two-inch wire as you did on the sides.

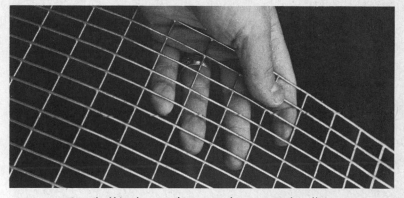

One-half inch strands are up, for a smoother floor.

Cut a door opening a foot square on one wide side (which will be the front), leaving half-inch stubs. Bend the stubs back with pliers so there will be no sharp edges. The door, also cut from one-inch by two-inch welded wire mesh, should overlap at least an inch all the way around. Many rabbit raisers prefer a door hinged at the top (with clips or rings) that swings up and into the cage. This is the way I build mine and the way commercial rabbitries want theirs, because this way the door is inside the hutch when open and not extending out into the aisle between hutches where it catches sleeves or otherwise gets in the way. Another good thing about this kind of door is that if you forget to latch it, it is still closed and prevents escape. Latches and hangers for holding the door up in the cage can be purchased for just a few cents from equipment suppliers, or you can make them yourself. A dog leash snap fastener also makes a good latch. In the accompanying photo, the door is shown swinging out and to the side. A wire hook latch made from a coat hanger holds it shut. Of course, these hutches may be ordered by mail. They arrive flat and are easily assembled with no cutting or measuring needed. Chances are that even purchasing them already built will cost you less than if you bought lumber to build hutches, unless your uncle owns the lumberyard.

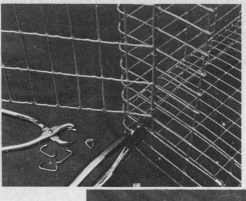

Hinged door overlaps the opening.

Dutch Rabbit relaxes in a new cage.

If you have this hutch indoors, perhaps in a garage or shed, you'll want to put a metal pan or a cardboard box lined with plastic sheeting underneath it to catch the droppings. Outdoors it will need a roof and sides of hardboard or plywood which you can fasten on with twisted wire, and perhaps a plastic or canvas curtain for cold days that you will hang on the front. Add legs to raise it off the ground. I've used one-by-three or two-by-two lumber and screw hooks to accomplish this. You might want to build the legs and roof together in table fashion and hang the hutch with hooks from it. The legs should be high enough to put the hutch at a convenient level for you to feed and water the rabbits, but also above splashback from rain and the depth of snow. Make sure your rabbits are out of the wind in winter and in the shade in summer. If your hutches are outside, try to locate them inside a shady plot protected from dogs (which can be a problem if they roam free, particularly in packs) by a high, sturdy fence. All-wire hutches can be suspended from a strong chain link or board fence, eliminating the need for legs and perhaps back wall weather protection. Make every effort to supply shade.

Housing And Equipment

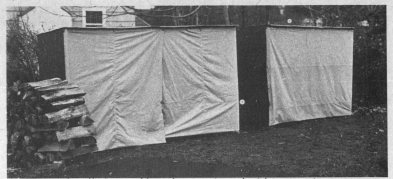

A group of well-situated hutches equipped with protective canvas.

A double roof, with about three or four inches between layers, is good protection from the sun if you don't have shade trees. Some raisers grow squash or pumpkin vines over their hutches to provide shade.

If you have space available in a well-ventilated shed or garage, your rabbits will be safe and you and they will be more comfortable in all kinds of weather. You may also want to consider a shed of some sort to keep your rabbits out of sight if you have neighbors who might be concerned about rabbits. While rabbits have no diseases they could possibly communicate to humans, some persons are not convinced, and have great imaginations. A shed or at least a fence keeps the rabbits out of sight and out of mind. A hedge is also good for this purpose.

If you do put your hutches inside a building, they are best over a dirt floor. A barn is great, and may have such a floor, but some breeders keep their rabbits in other kinds of outbuildings, even the garage. My own are in a specially constructed steel shed that was built from two prefabricated steel storage buildings that I modified to provide extra ventilation. The photo on page 115 shows this building. Many garden sheds are on the market today which would provide good housing for rabbits. In addition, there are several plans for pole buildings (see Garden Way's pole building book) and small barns. Chicken coops no longer in use may be reactivated. A good friend of mine built the sheds shown in the photos here, and they serve him well.

They show how he built sheds for his rabbits from perforated steel angle iron which goes together like a child's construction set. Except for sheathing, no wood is used.

This angle iron is a very versatile framing material that requires only nuts and bolts for assembly. Not only does it support the shed structure, but it is also sufficient to hold the weight of the hutches and rabbits inside.

The material is called Dexion. An ordinary hex wrench and a Dexion cutter (the cutter may be borrowed or rented from the distributor or retailer) are all that is needed. Measurement is easy as there are diamond-shaped marks appearing every three inches as a guide. Just count the diamonds. We found that a nut driver (similar to a screwdriver but with a hex socket head to fit the nuts) was very handy for holding the hex bolt.

Perforated angle iron stock bolts together (below) to form a sturdy support frame (at left) for six rabbit cages. Plans for this shed are shown on pp 151-54.

Measure carefully, then cut all the pieces. Another pair of hands will help when assembling the basic frame. S-hooks were used to hang the wire cages from the frame. Galvanized sheet metal was used for dropping boards. A good pitch front to back is necessary so droppings will roll to the rear and fall to the ground. Make sure you leave enough room in front between the cage bottom and the dropping pan to use a scraper or hoe occasionally. Because Dexion is steel, it does not rot in contact with the ground. It can be bolted to footings or treated wooden members such as railroad ties, perhaps buried underground. If

high winds are no problem, merely setting it on bricks or concrete blocks probably will suffice. The Dexion frames were covered with exterior grade plywood bolted directly onto the frame. The roofs were shingled and were built with a couple of feet of front overhang to protect the rabbit keeper as he tended the rabbits, and also to keep the sun off the animals.

A cleanout panel in back, hinged 18 inches off the ground, is handy. A single unit may be used with a rollup canvas in front or two may face each other. We used a white fiberglass skylight roof over the facing units, and a more extensive use of fiberglass could be used in sheathing. White fiberglass admits light but reflects heat. It also lets you view the rabbits in a more natural light than does the green fiberglass. Clear fiberglass admits more light but also heat. It's great for greenhouses, but if you use it for hutch sheds you may have roast rabbit on the hoof. One nice thing worth adding about the Dexion is that you can add extensions at later dates by simply bolting on more sections to the existing ones. And if you should decide to house your rabbits another way, or simply get rid of them, the whole thing can be taken apart and used for shelving in the garage or basement, even for a workbench frame. I don't sell this stuff, but I am sold on it.

While Dexion was used, and this material is available all over the country, there are other brands of angle iron that will do as well. You might consider using old steel shelving framing members if you can obtain some. Often the classified pages of the local newspaper will reveal that some warehouse is selling out. Unperforated steel angle iron, obtainable used from a junkyard, is also good if you have a heavy duty electric drill to make the holes for the bolts. Wood may be used, and if treated against rot the way fence posts are, will do the job. Plenty of paint will also help, but some maintenance of this sort will be needed in the future, while the steel won't require as much attention.

Sheds such as these help create an environment for rabbits that is easy to keep clean. People like clean rabbits in clean surroundings, particularly if they live next door to them — or if they plan to buy them.

Depending upon how many hutches you plan to have, a shed may prove cheaper to construct in the long run than the protection of individual hutches. But no matter how you protect them, make certain that the hutches are easily removable. They can receive an occasional hosing off and disinfecting this way, and the inside of the shed is more accesssible for painting. Also, should you decide to hang larger or smaller hutches inside at a later date, because of possible switch to larger or smaller breeds, you will be able to do so easily. For versatility the all-wire hutch simply has no equal.

Manufactured type of suspended cages hang from roof rafters.

Self-stacking cages from Favorite Manufacturing Co.

OTHER EQUIPMENT

What else do you need inside your hutch besides rabbits? Three things only: A feeder, a waterer and a removable nest box where the young will be born. Of course you don't need a nest box for each hutch as they can be rotated when and where needed. The young stay in the box only three to four weeks.

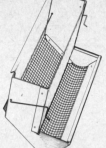

Screened bottom of self-feeder allows dust in the pellets to fall through. Self-waterer and feeder are used in the cage below.

FEEDER

I know a rabbit raiser who uses a one pound coffee can for a feeder. He says he can't afford to use a galvanized metal self-feeder as I do and as is illustrated on the hutches shown in the photo. The self-feeder costs less than $2, depending upon the size, as they come in varying widths. The man who can't afford to buy this feeder should look under his hutch. There he would find enough wasted feed to pay for the feeder — maybe one made of sterling silver.

The rabbits tip the coffee can over, or scratch out the feed when they don't. They are given two to three times as much feed as they need, and yet they don't get enough to eat and are underweight. While droppings fall through the floor of the wire hutch, so do rabbit pellets and grains.

The self-feeder, which attaches to the outside of the hutch, has a lip on the rim of the trough to prevent scratching feed out, and of course it can't be tipped over. Furthermore, it takes up no space on the hutch floor, which allows you to build your all-wire hutch smaller than a wooden one would have to be. Also, it can be loaded from the outside of the hutch, without opening the door. Rabbits cannot easily foul it because they can't sit in it, so the feed stays clean. It holds enough for a couple of days in case you have to be away. There are some earthenware crocks to be found that won't tip over and some have a lip to prevent scratching out the feed. But they do take up floor space and constantly are in need of cleaning (which means soiled and wasted feed). And so the metal self-feeder gets my vote.

WATERER

For a number of years I used earthenware crocks to water my rabbits. Again, a tin can tips over and the rabbits go thirsty. Of course, it also rusts. Rabbits need clean, fresh water at all times to grow well. A crock doesn't really provide this, and it needs a lot of rinsing and washing, but it comes a lot closer than tin cans. If you use a crock, look for one that has a smaller interior diameter at the bottom than at the top. Otherwise, in winter if the water freezes, you will be left with a cracked or broken crock, because the water expands when it becomes ice.

When I discovered the dew drop watering valve, I packed my crocks away in the garage. This little valve, which is shown in the photo, costs only 35 or 45 cents, a lot less than a crock. It was designed to be inserted into a pipe carrying water from a tank to the hutches, and that's the way I use them now, in a manner I will soon describe. But first I used them without the pipe, inserted into plastic jugs such as contain laundry bleach, or milk, in some localities. When inserted into the jug and hung from the outside of the hutch with the valve protruding into it, the dew drop waterer is very handy and inexpensive. Note that the top of the jug is left off to allow air. The rabbit simply bites on the end of the dew drop valve, which has a little stem inside it that retracts to let the water trickle into the animal's mouth. When he stops biting, the stem drops down, the valve closes and the water stops, except perhaps for an intermittent "dew drop" which provides the device a name.

It is a simple matter to insert the valve into the jug by cutting a small hole with a knife and pressing the valve into place. Epoxy cement keeps it from leaking and falling out. You can use the gallon or half-gallon jugs and thus provide plenty of drinking water that stays fresh and clean. In fact, it holds enough so you only have to replenish it every other day instead of every day, as with a crock. If you should be away for a day, nobody has to water your rabbits for you.

The little dew drop valve does a fine job with a jug, but an even better one attached to a pipe. Cold water flexible plastic pipe costs only pennies per foot and can be tapped to accept these dew drop valves. The pipe runs behind the all-wire hutch, with a small opening cut in the wire about 10 inches above the floor to give the rabbits access and allow them to drink. Pipes may be purchased already drilled or tapped and cut to length, or you can do it yourself with ease. I had no prior experience with this pipe when I put together a completely automatic watering system for my rabbits.

Once you have established the ultimate number of hutches you expect to have, you can plan an automatic or a semi-automatic watering system. An automatic system, such as mine, utilizes water piped in from the city water system, into a breaker tank which reduces the pressure, and then down through the pipes to the valves in the hutches. A semi-automatic system features a holding tank, which might be a jerry jug or even a big pail, with the pipe leading to the hutches. You have to fill the holding tank yourself, perhaps with a hose, but you don't have to fill individual jugs or crocks (and you don't have to rinse and wash them).

Cold weather complicates watering. If you use crocks, the best thing to do is fill them only halfway in the morning, let the rabbits drink, and either dump them out or let the water stand and freeze. Then, at night, fill them the rest of the way and hope the rabbits get a good drink before they start licking ice. The next day you take the crock inside, or put it into a bucket of hot water to remove the ice. This is a nuisance, but must be done. It's nice to have two crocks for every hutch so one can thaw while the other is in use. This can be expensive, with crocks costing a couple of dollars a piece or more these days. If you can use the jugs with valves, you can provide two for each hutch, alternately using one and thawing the other, and the price comes way down, because two valves cost less than half as much as one crock.

With a semi-automatic or an automatic piped system, you can insert into the pipe an electrical heating cable that will keep the water from freezing. You simply thread it through the pipe after it is tapped but before you insert the dew drop valves. The two ends are fastened to a plug which you can attach to a heavy duty extension cord and run to the house or garage electricity and plug in when needed. Mine is actually a permanent electrical installation and uses a thermostat

Automatic watering system is a great labor saver.

which cost about $8 and has returned its price many times. When the temperature goes down to 32 degrees, the cable goes on automatically. Thus, the cable is not on when it's not needed but is activated when necessary. In my rabbitry I have two cables inside the pipe. One is attached to the thermostat, comes on at 32 degrees, and protects the water from freezing down to about zero. The second cable is manually plugged in when the temperature falls below zero, which occurs only occasionally in New Jersey, and it protects the water down to probably 25 below, although it doesn't get that cold around here.

This cable provides about 2½ watts of heat per foot and because my two cables are about 100 feet long, only 250 watts are required to keep the water from freezing in my 36 hutches. It could be 500 watts on severe nights, but in the past three years the temperature hasn't fallen low enough to use both cables.

You could of course simply drain the pipes on cold nights, particularly if you live where freezing temperatures are rare. You could use crocks or jugs at those times. With plastic pipe there is no need to fear breakage if water should freeze within, because the plastic expands to accommodate the ice. Of course, if your rabbits are indoors, you could heat the building. One way or another you can keep your rabbits watered.

Complete directions for installation of piped water systems can be obtained from suppliers of the pipes and valves and other equipment. I think you definitely should explore the use of a piped system if you have as many as a dozen hutches. Most of the time required to take care of rabbits is in the watering and cleaning of crocks. Should you be able to plan your complete rabbitry from the outset, it is a simple matter to install automatic watering at that time. It's a bit difficult to do in stages. But if you can do it all at first, you will be able to provide an automatic watering system for less than the cost of crocks. And you and your rabbits will be better off.

NEST BOX

The only other equipment you really need is a nest box for the doe and litter. This can be constructed of light plywood or a metal box can be purchased. Perhaps you will be able to find an apple box that you can adapt to do the job. A box 18 inches long, 10 inches wide and 10 inches high is big enough for all but the giant breeds, which need a box about 15 inches wide and two feet long. Make certain that the box will fit through the hutch door. Don't build or buy a covered box. These are damp, which can be fatal to young rabbits. I don't care how cold it gets where you are, an open box is better than a closed one.

A popular style of box is one made of welded wire, such as used on the floor of rabbit hutches, and lined with cardboard in cold weather (see photo). Don't use a cardboard box alone, however, as it may turn over and the nest would be destroyed and the babies along with it. It would also be chewed to pieces in short order. You always have a clean, new cardboard liner with this kind of box. In warm weather you use cardboard only on the bottom, letting air circulate through the wire mesh sides. I have found that the wire nest box, like the wire cage, is the most satisfactory and I now use it exclusively. I bought some and built some myself.

Wire nest box with 3-week-old rabbits has cardboard liner.

In summary, you can see that the ideal situation is all-wire hutches inside a building if possible, at least inside a fence, and also galvanized metal self-feeders and some use of the dew drop water valve. All these items are carried by several equipment manufacturers who are eager to ship them to you.

You should write for their catalogs, using the names and addresses found at the back of this book. Study these catalogs and see what is offered. There are variations in quality. You get what you pay for, so sometimes a higher price will deliver better goods, but almost everything they offer will do the job. I have made purchases from just about every one of them from time to time. You will get a lot of good ideas from these catalogs and I urge you to pore over them before you build your rabbitry.

5
Feeding Rabbits Right

Everyone knows what rabbits eat, right? Cabbage and carrots and plenty of 'em, right?

Wrong!

There are plenty of things that rabbits *will* eat, including the salad mentioned above, but to be successful with rabbits, or any other livestock, you must feed them what they *should* eat.

Just as nutritionists have determined what humans should eat, livestock nutritionists have concluded that rabbits need a balanced diet to grow and reproduce. Because you will be trying to put your rabbits in the best of health for the best growth and reproduction, you will want to feed them the optimum ration.

IT USED TO BE A TOUGH JOB

Many years ago it was a difficult task to gather all the feed grains and roots and roughage that rabbits need. But now feed manufacturers, backed by staffs of degreed professional research nutritionists, have assembled all the ingredients for rabbit raisers. And they have sacked them up for you in the form of the bite-size rabbit pellet.

PELLETS MAKE IT EASY NOW

The pellets in this sack got there only on the basis of a complete understanding of what the rabbit requires. The pellets contain everything the rabbit needs:
- Alfalfa hay for high quality roughage,
- Special sources of protein, including some of animal origin,
- Phosphorous, calcium, essential trace minerals and
- Sources of necessary vitamins.

Protein levels of these pellets range from 16 to 18 per cent, which is necessary for milk production in the doe bringing up a litter and for the growing rabbit.

THE RESEARCH GOES ON

The major feed companies conduct continual experiments in research farms and laboratories and have advanced the feeding of rabbits to an extremely high degree. Mortality of young rabbits has been reduced tremendously from the days before pellets — and the growth rate has zoomed.

The protein content and the ingredients of different brands of pellets may vary slightly; in fact, the contents of the same brand may vary from feed mill to feed mill. But all the varieties are good and one thing is certain:

If all you ever give your rabbits are pellets to eat and clean water to drink, you and they will be doing fine.

In spite of all the iron-clad evidence that pellets are the best feed for rabbits, there still are those who insist upon feeding rabbits something else. And, of course, rabbits can exist and even thrive on other feeds, although the odds are that they won't. You might think you could feed rabbits for less money than pellets cost, but it is not very likely if you consider death losses, longer times to market weight, poor quality carcasses, and fewer and smaller litters. In addition, quite often non-pelleted feed is wasted because of spoilage or because rabbits scratch it out of feeders (sometimes, as in the case of mixed grains, they prefer what's down under to what's on top).

YOU CAN COMPLICATE YOUR LIFE

You can make feeding rabbits a complicated affair with unpredictable results, or you can make it a simple thing that you can count on to make your rabbits perform the way you hope they will. If you feed pellets, it is a simple matter to calculate how much to feed and when. If you feed anything else, it is a difficult task to judge the amount because it's not easy to measure.

While I strongly urge you to feed pellets, I'm not averse to supplementing them with other items, but these must be used judiciously. You're better off not trying them until you get used to your rabbits for a while. They will complicate your feeding schedule, but there are times when they can help you, depending upon your objectives and what is available to you.

Here are some general requirements for feed: For dry does, herd bucks and developing young, you should provide a ration that has at least 12 to 15 per cent protein, 2 to 3.5 per cent fat and 20 to 27 per cent fiber. For pregnant does and does with litters, the percentages of the ration should include: protein, 16 to 20 per cent; fat, 3 to 5.5 per cent, and fiber, 15 to 20 per cent.

You can put together your own feed based on these guidelines, and you can do it by using three sources: dry roughages, green roughages (including roots and tubers) and concentrates.

Dry roughages include alfalfa hay, clover hay, lespedeza hay, oat hay, peanut hay, soybean, timothy and vetch hay. Greens that provide sources of rabbit feed are carrots (roots), rutabagas, sweet potatoes and turnips, along with lettuce. Cabbage could be included but it's very gassy and can be a killer.

Among the concentrates are barley, beet pulp (dried), bread, brewers' grains, buckwheat, corn, cottonseed and linseed meals, milk, oats, peanut meal, sorghum meal, soybean meal and wheat. If you like, you can mix up a ration from these items, naturally calculating the percentage of protein, roughage and fat they will deliver to your rabbits. You should actually feed them in a feeder with separate compartments, or in separate dishes, because the rabbits are likely to scratch them out and waste them if you don't. Some of the grains will have to be ground, cracked or rolled. Then again, you have to watch out how much the rabbits eat. They have individual preferences and some will eat more of one thing than they should and less of another. Greens should be thoroughly washed, because you never know what they might have been sprayed with. (Please don't *ever* feed greens to young rabbits as it will give them diarrhea.)

The former president of the American Rabbit Breeders Assn., Oren Reynolds, who lives in Illinois, has shared with the members his practice of supplementing rabbit pellets with a special mixture that he feels does a good job for him. Mr. Reynolds has for many years been one of the nation's very best rabbit breeders so if you are interested in making the effort to feed rabbits the way he does, here's how it goes:

Mix six quarts of oats, one quart of wheat, one quart of sunflower seed, one quart of barley (whole if available, otherwise crimped) and one quart of kaffir corn when it is available. Add a quart of Terramycin crumbles to the feed once a week. Feed one part of this mixture to three parts of pellets daily.

"Since I'm retired and have time," says Mr. Reynolds, "I feed the pellets at night and the grain in the morning. They can be fed together but some animals like one ingredient better than others and will scratch out the other feed to get to it."

WHAT KIND OF HAY?

Alfalfa hay is my first choice, and I feed it when I can get it. I add it to the usual amount of pellets and I know the rabbits enjoy it even though they get a lot of it in the pellet. If they didn't clean up all their pellets, they wouldn't get the hay. Almost any other fine-stemmed, leafy, green, well-cured hay that is free from mildew or mold will do nicely. Cut it into short lengths to cut down waste.

HOW TO SIMPLIFY YOUR LIFE

Rabbit pellets supply all the dietary needs of your rabbits, so why let them fill up on feed that doesn't do the complete job? You wouldn't munch on candy all day and expect to be well nourished. So think of greens, carrots, leftover dry bread and other items that might be used sporadically as you think of candy — tasty morsels used sparingly as treats.

Here's how I feed my rabbits and how I think you should feed yours if you want to achieve success with them. Remember, feeding has the single most important influence on your rabbits' well-being.

THE DOE AND HER LITTER

I provide the doe and her litter with all the rabbit pellets they want. This means I keep the self-feeder loaded to the point where they never run out. I want the young to have all they want because (a) they should grow as fast as they can, and (b) the doe needs to keep up her milk supply while the litter is nursing. In addition to hay as a supplement, I sometimes feed whole oats — the best I can get. These are usually called race horse oats and are sold by the 50 pound bag. I feed these in a separate feeder, or on one side of my wide self-feeders. When the litter pops out of the nest box, this is the time to add oats. Lots of successful breeders add oats to keep the young growing well, particularly if it's an unusually large litter or if they plan to rebreed the doe earlier than normal (which I'll get into a little bit later). I also feed the litter a creep feed. This consists of a tiny pellet just the right size for the babies. It contains 22 per cent protein, 5 per cent fat and 12 per cent fiber. I feed this in a special creep feeder that admits the young but prevents the doe from eating it. I feed this creep feed only when the litter is extra large, or the doe is one that doesn't have a very good milk supply, or when I plan to rebreed her early.

Special creep feeder's small openings to the feed hopper admit the baby rabbits but keep the doe from the tiny, high-protein pellets. Regular pellets for the doe are shown in the top of this divided hopper.

THE PREGNANT DOE

My does aren't pregnant until I palpate them, a procedure I'll describe in the next chapter. Of course they really are, but I don't know it. So until I know it, I consider them quite un-pregnant. And that means I limit the amount of pellets they get. Until a full-grown, adult doe is pregnant, she gets only enough feed to keep her slim and trim. I don't want her fat for two reasons. First, if she really isn't pregnant, extra internal fat can choke off the fallopian tubes, stop the descent of her eggs and thus prevent conception. Second, if she really is expecting, extra fat can make delivery difficult and could even kill her.

My does, the Tans, get about two ounces a day of pellets until I know they are pregnant. Then they get another ounce if they will clean it up, and they get about a tablespoonful of oats and another tablespoonful of calf pellets. These calf pellets, sold under the trade name of Calf Manna, offer 25 per cent protein, 3 per cent fat and 6 per cent fiber. They are loaded with vitamins and minerals, in addition to feeding oat meal, soybean meal, corn, dried whey, linseed meal, hominy feed, dehydrated alfalfa meal, dextrose, fish meal, animal liver and glandular meal, ground limestone, salt and dried brewers yeast. I'm convinced that Calf Manna improves the milk flow and otherwise conditions my doe to deliver a healthy, lively litter of babies.

ON THE DAY OF DELIVERY

When this doe delivers her litter, or kindles as the rabbit men call it, she gets all the items mentioned above, but she also qualifies for the special treats I have mentioned. I offer her a slice of apple, or a carrot, or a few leaves of lettuce, the tops of the celery, a few potato peelings or something of this sort (except cabbage leaves, which I loathe because of the gassy aspect). This doe is of course very thirsty and so in addition to the water that all my rabbits have access to continuously, such a morsel of greens or roots is quite well received. I may continue to give her a bit of feed of this kind daily until the litter comes hopping out of the nest box. Then it ceases (although I've been known to feed a bit of it out of my hand to the doe) because I don't want the youngsters to get hold of any greens. Remember young Peter Rabbit? He returned home to a sickbed after his escape from Mr. MacGregor's garden. Outside of an upset stomach, all you can possibly do by feeding greens to three-week-old rabbits is kill them.

WHAT TO FEED THE WEANLINGS

When I wean the litter, which I do at six to ten weeks (and which I'll elaborate upon in the next chapter), I give them all the rabbit pellets they will clean up in one day. I don't let any feed hang around in the dish and get stale and moldy, by any means. But I make sure that these young, growing animals get all they can put away. If they do not seem to be gaining as well as they should, I give some oats, and of course, I always give hay when I can get good alfalfa. I particularly like to give hay to the youngsters, and I believe that you really can't overdo the roughage on the young. It seems to me that the more roughage you give the youngsters the less chance they have of getting diarrhea, which can be a problem with young rabbits. I NEVER give any greens to rabbits less than five or six months of age under any circumstances. They won't do a bit of good and can, of course, kill them. There simply isn't any percentage in giving greens to young rabbits.

WHAT TO FEED THE BUCK

I give my bucks about two ounces of rabbit pellets per day. These are Tans, remember, which are small rabbits. I'll give you some general guidelines for all sizes of rabbits, but the main thing to remember about feeding bucks is to keep them slim and trim. I don't know if it makes any sense to say it, but I don't like to satiate the appetite of the buck, because I want him to retain his appetite for romance. A breeder buck that sits around in the corner like Ferdinand the Bull with no sexual appetite isn't going to do me any good. If I fill him up so he's fat and lazy I don't think he'll chase females. So I keep him in loving trim.

WHAT TO FEED THE JUNIORS

Junior does, those developing does who are older than weanlings — oh, about 4, 5 or 6 months old, just too young to breed, get a measured amount of feed that will keep them on the slim side, too. If they are too fat they won't conceive, or if they do, they might have trouble on the day of delivery. So their pellets are limited to about two ounces a day.

I don't worry too much about junior bucks. For one thing, they don't have to kindle a litter. So I let them eat about all they will clean up in a day. But I certainly don't let any feed hang around from day to day.

WHO ELSE IS THERE?

Well, there are those rabbits that you plan to show. Conditioning a rabbit for a show is a whole special ball game that I'll cover in Chapter

10. This is a chapter where I violate all the rules I lay down in this chapter — where I feed all kinds of things in addition to rabbit pellets; where I feed all the things that the top winners for years have fed their champions. It's the chapter where I put a keen edge on the rabbits — an edge that can dull quickly but one that when sharp will cut the competition down.

SOME GENERAL GUIDELINES

Young, growing rabbits should be fed all the rabbit pellets they will eat in a day. You will soon find out how much to feed. A lot depends upon the size and age of your rabbits. If feed is left over the following day, give less. If the rabbit greets you at feeding time by diving head-long into his feed, you will want to give him more. Adult rabbits of the medium weight group consume about five ounces of rabbit pellets a day; again, more or less, depending upon the individual. Females with litters should have pellets before them at all times. Clean, fresh water must be available constantly. Watch out for overly fat does. Lazy bucks are probably overfed. In fact, most rabbits are probably overfed. Except for does with litters, rabbits do *not* need feed in front of them constantly. My adult bucks, and does without litters usually clean up all their pellets within an hour and that's all they get until the next day.

Of course, they almost always have hay to munch on, probably more for something to do, although they enjoy it, than because they need it.

SHARP EYE NEEDED AT FEEDING TIME

A good rabbit raiser keeps a close watch on his stock at feeding time. He also runs his hand over each rabbit at that time if he possibly can. One that's a bit bony gets more. If your rabbit hasn't cleaned up his pellets, something is wrong. First, check the water supply. Is the crock or jug empty? Is the valve plugged? Rabbits don't eat when they are thirsty. To get them eating and growing well they must have plenty of water. Most of the time a rabbit who isn't eating isn't drinking. Note the droppings under the hutch. They should be large and round — well-formed. This is a good time to watch out for diarrhea. If a rabbit is off-feed, simply not eating well and he is apparently healthy, try tempting him with a tidbit of dry bread, or a leaf of lettuce or a spoonful of oats. This will usually get him back to the feeder.

WHEN TO FEED

If there is one best time of day to feed rabbits, it's in the evening. They are more active at night and will eat more readily when day is done. But if morning is more convenient, your rabbits will adjust to your good schedule. Rabbits do, however, require regularity. If evening is your choice, then feed them regularly every evening. Don't make your rabbits wait to be fed, and don't feed them early just because you happened to get home a little sooner. Many livestockmen like to feed their animals before they sit down to their own evening meal.

If you use water crocks, rinse them daily and disinfect weekly. This routine, in an all-wire hutch that keeps itself clean, will do much to keep your rabbits healthy.

In Chapter 8 I'll cover some feeds that you can produce yourself in your garden to supplement pellet feeding. There are good opportunities among garden crops to stretch your pellets, particularly with dry does and bucks you are only trying to maintain, in the event that your freezer is already full of dressed rabbit and you're not yet ready for more.

WHAT ABOUT SALT?

The question of how and when to feed salt often leads to confusion. If you need a commercial brand of rabbit pellets salt will be in them. I haven't fed salt in years. If you use a salt spool it might corrode your hutch. If you really must add salt, I'd sprinkle it right from a shaker onto the pellets or other feed.

WHAT ELSE CAN I TELL YOU?

There's nothing as important as good feed and feeding practice. You can't go wrong with pellets and the choice between them and a home-mixed feed depends mostly on what you can obtain and how much time you have to prepare it. If you are a beginner, I can't urge you too strongly to stick to pellets. As you gain experience you may try other feeds.

6
Managing
Rabbits Right

If you have started right so far, you have chosen a breed, obtained foundation stock and housed them in all-wire hutches, happily munching pellets. You have done a lot for them so far. But what have they done for you lately?

Probably what they have been doing, if you have been taking good care of them, is growing to breeding age. Now they are ready to start producing for you.

MATING YOUR RABBITS

To get into production, you must mate that first pair. For the small breeds, your does and bucks should be at least five months of age. The medium breeds should be six months and the giants must be at least eight months of age. For my Tans, a small breed, I always say five months or five pounds, which ever comes first.

LOOK 'EM OVER

Let's assume you have decided which buck and which doe are to be mated, based upon objectives of your breeding program, which we soon will cover. For now, let's agree that you have chosen two specimens from which you wish to produce a litter. First, look at the doe. She should be at just the right weight. Not too fat. Her fur condition should be excellent — no shedding and plenty of sheen. Now, check the vulva. For best results it should be a reddish purple color — not a pale pink. If it has the deep color, this doe probably is ready to breed, provided she is otherwise in perfect health.

Now look at the buck. His fur too should be in good condition — his coat should shine, indicating his health is good. His eyes should be bright, another indicator. Whether he is fat or thin is not so important as it is for the doe, but if he is too fat he may be too lazy to service the doe.

Next, check his testicles. If they are completely descended into the scrotum, and the scrotum is full and large, he is a good buck to use. If he has only one testicle, or if one or both are withdrawn into the groin or have a withered look, he may be sterile, or if a litter results it may be small. This condition may be only temporary. One testicle may not yet have descended into the scrotum. Or, the withered, wrinkled look may be seasonal — it happens particularly to older bucks in late summer and autumn. But it is terribly important to check this out, to make sure you get the litter you want. If you want reproduction, make certain the reproductive apparatus is in perfect working order — at least as far as you can see.

TAKE THE DOE TO THE BUCK

If both prospective parents look just right to you, take the doe to the buck's hutch and put her in. Never take the buck to the doe. And never simply leave the pair alone together. Put the doe in with the buck and observe the mating.

Don't blink, or you may miss it. Rabbits are rabbits. They mate like rabbits. If everything goes right, and it usually does, it will be all over before you close the hutch door. The buck will have mounted the doe. The doe will have raised her hind quarters. The buck will have serviced the doe and fallen over backwards or on his side.

Now remove the doe. Turn her over and check the vulva to make sure the semen has been deposited there. There's nothing like seeing for believing. Leave nothing to chance.

WHAT ABOUT A CYCLE?

Is it really just this simple? Usually, but not always. It has been reported that the female rabbit has no cycle, that she is fertile 365 days of the year. It has also been reported that the female rabbit is fertile for 12 days, followed by 2-4 days during which she will not conceive, followed by another dozen days when she will. Either way, cycle or not, she will conceive most of the time. And either way, who knows which days are which?

If a doe rabbit has a cycle, you really aren't going to know when she is fertile or infertile anyway. So I say, forget it. It is known that the doe rabbit's eggs descend for fertilization upon sexual stimulation. In other words, after service. This process is said to take eight to ten hours, at which time the eggs meet the sperm and conception takes place. This assumes that the sperm is there. If the doe should urinate in the meantime, the semen may be washed away.

PUT HER BACK IN WITH THE BUCK

So, what I do is put her back in the buck's hutch eight to ten hours later. If the eggs are descending, now's the time for conception. The buck, of course, is ready, and another service may be just what is needed, particularly if the semen from the first service is no longer in the uterus. This is something you won't really know unless you stand around and watch for eight hours. Like me, you probably have something else to do.

SUPPOSE NOTHING HAPPENS

Okay, you have put the doe in with the buck for the first time, but no mating occurs. Either he sits in the corner like Ferdinand the Bull and pays her no mind, or he chases her like crazy but she resists these advances with unparalleled virtue. You have a problem, but not an insurmountable one, to be sure.

If the buck is not interested, try another if you have one. The second is almost certain to service the doe. Finding two unwilling buck rabbits in a row is almost unheard of. But what if you have only one?

If the doe is willing and the buck is not, try this: Pick the buck up and put him on the doe's back. He probably will get the idea. If that doesn't work, leave the doe in his hutch, but take him out. Put him in hers and leave them there overnight. He will pick up her scent and by the next day doubtless will be more interested. At that time, bring her back to her own hutch, put her in and the buck will probably service her. She also should be more interested, having acquired his scent. If this doesn't work, the buck probably is too fat and lazy. You can start to slim him down by reducing his feed intake, but in the meantime attempt the mating *before* you feed the buck. Try the morning or the evening before he dives into his pellets.

WHAT ABOUT THE DOE?

What is more likely by far is that the doe will show no interest. For every buck that isn't ready, 100 does are not. She may hunch down in a corner of the buck's hutch. She may flatten right down on the floor. She may climb one wall. She may resist every advance instead of raising her hind quarters and lifting her tail to accept the buck.

There are a number of ways to get this doe bred. In my many years of rabbit raising, I still haven't seen the doe I can't get bred! It may take a while, but they will breed. Surely, there are those nature has not completely equipped for reproduction. Certainly, it can happen. But it hasn't happened to my rabbits yet. I hate to repeat it so often, but rabbits are rabbits are rabbits. They will out-produce almost anything.

So here's how to handle the uncooperative doe. First, you might leave her in the buck's hutch overnight, removing him of course to her quarters. She will acquire his smell, which is apt to put her in the mood. The next day take her back to her own hutch, where the buck is waiting. She will probably accept service at this time.

Here's something to keep in mind. Sometimes when you put the doe in with the buck she will run from him and act as though she has no interest in mating whatsoever. But watch her tail. If she twitches her tail, you can be sure you are seeing a coy doe playing hard to get. A doe whose tail is twitching is a doe who's itching for romance. She may run for awhile, but sooner or later she wants to be caught.

FORCED MATINGS

But, where the buck is willing (99 per cent of the time) and the doe is not (occasionally), I restrain the doe for a forced mating. I place her in the buck's hutch, rear end first and grab her by the loose flesh over the shoulders (the scruff of the neck) with one hand and slide the other under her belly. I place the thumb and forefinger on either side of the vulva, pushing gently toward the rear and lifting slightly. The buck will mount the doe, which is in a receptive position, and the service will take place. Sometimes, in the case of a reluctant pair, I have restrained the doe, picked up the buck and put him over her, and held her for him.

Let me offer this final warning: Never leave the pair together unattended! They might fight and injure each other and you'll never know if and when she is bred.

GREAT, SHE'S PREGNANT!

Just because a mating has taken place, and just because they are rabbits, don't start counting bunnies until they are born. Conception may not have taken place. But how do you know for sure?

There are a couple of ways of telling, and one is more certain than the other. First, however, I would weigh the doe at mating time, and record the poundage. Later, if she has gained a significant amount on the same feed that previously had maintained her at a given figure, she probably is pregnant. If, for example, she weighs an additional pound in two weeks (for the medium weight breeds), she probably is pregnant. But you really can't be sure.

Two weeks after you have mated the pair, place the doe back in the buck's hutch. If she resists his advances and also growls and whines and generally complains, it's a good *bet* she is pregnant. But it's only a good bet. It's not a certainty. If she weighs another pound it's a better bet, but you still can't be sure.

On the other hand, let's suppose she does not resist the buck, or even if she does you restrain her for a forced mating and the buck completes a service. Record the date, because she may now be bred if she isn't already pregnant, and you will have saved yourself half the gestation period.

BUT HOW DO YOU TELL FOR SURE?

You're still not certain she's in a family way, right? Okay, ten days to two weeks after mating, try palpation — feeling for the young. Pick the doe up and place her on a flat surface, perhaps on a feed sack on a table. Hold her by the scruff of the neck with one hand and slide the other under her belly. Feel around gently for signs of life. Within ten days or two weeks, the youngsters on the way feel like large marbles slightly to both sides of center in the belly, just forward of the groin area. For comparison, feel another doe you know is not pregnant, or even a buck. Palpation does take practice, but it's the only sure way to tell if your does are pregnant.

Test mating, putting the doe back in with the buck to test her reaction, isn't conclusive because some does will complain and growl even if they aren't pregnant, and some won't even if they are. After a while, however, you will learn from your rabbits (if you are observant) which ones will complain when they are. Test mating works for sure with some does, but you have to know which ones. This takes time and watchfulness.

YOU'RE STILL NOT CERTAIN?

Now you think you feel those large marbles. She has gained a pound. She growls like mad when you put her back in with the buck. Three and a half weeks of the 28-34-day gestation period have passed. Throw a handful of straw on the hutch floor. If all the other tests have proved positive, and she starts picking up the straw in her mouth and carrying it around, I'll bet you anything she is pregnant.

TIME FOR THE NEST BOX

The gestation period is 28 to 34 days, but most bunnies are born on the 31st day. On the 27th day it's time to put in the nest box. You want the doe to have the box in time to get used to it, in time to build her nest in it, but not too early. If it's there too soon, before she's overcome by the maternal nest-building impulse, she may use it for a bathroom. So wait until the 27th day after mating.

Earlier, in Chapter 4, I pointed out the necessity for providing a nest box with an open top. You might adapt an apple box, build one from light plywood, cage floor wire, or purchase either an open top metal box or a wire mesh box. My favorite is the wire mesh box lined with cardboard in the winter, left unlined when warm.

IN WARM WEATHER

During the warm months, with overnight temperatures in at least the fifties, place about an inch of shredded sugar cane in the bottom of the box, if you can find some. This stuff is trade-named Servall Staz-dry and is sold at feed stores. It is shredded, oven-dried sugar cane left over from the harvest. It is sterile and has an amazing advantage over wood shavings, which you can use if it's all you have. It remains dry on top if urinated in. This means that the nest will stay dry on the surface, next to the babies. Shavings are okay, but sawdust is not, as it can suffocate the young. On top of the shredded sugar cane or shavings, place handfuls of straw, filling up the box. This should be nice soft straw, not stemmy hay which will not mix as well with the fur in the nest.

IN THE WINTER

During the cold months, I line the box with cardboard. This is unnecessary with a wooden box, but a couple of layers in the bottom of a wooden box won't hurt. The corrugated cardboard provides insulation should the young burrow to the bottom. I use three to four inches of the Staz-dry for additional absorbency and warmth. Then I pack in all the straw I can, ramming my fist way down deep inside to make a cavern I hope the doe will burrow into to kindle her young. She sometimes will, but even if she rearranges it all, she needs plenty of straw in the nest in the winter.

By the thirty-first day, as a rule, the doe will kindle the litter in the box. If it's an extra large litter she may kindle on the 30th day. The vast majority of my does, of all the breeds I have raised, have kindled on the 31st. Rarely does the litter arrive after the 31st day, but don't give up hope until after the 34th.

HOW THE DOE MAKES A NEST

On the day the litter is born, more often the night, the doe will burrow into the straw, pull fur from her underside and build a nesting place for the young. After they are born, she will pull more fur and cover them up. If she does a good job of this, her litter will survive in below-zero weather. If she doesn't, they may perish in above-freezing temperatures. You can help her out, if she doesn't cover them well with fur, by plucking some from her yourself and covering the young. Or, you can save fur from the summer months when there is more than enough, and add it to the nest box in the winter. I have one doe who nearly denudes herself in July or August, but is reluctant to part with her fur in the winter. So I save it for use when needed.

INSPECTING THE LITTER

The doe needs peace and quiet a few days before the litter is born and a few days after. Dogs and children can be particularly disturbing at this time. You will of course be very curious to see the litter.

If you have placed the nest box in the back of the hutch but in full view from the front, you will be able to see into it, and by the 31st day you should see a pile of fluffy fur toward the rear of it, slightly moving up and down.

A litter of newborn rabbits secure in their snug nest box.

TIME FOR THE TIDBIT

Now's the time to bring out that lettuce leaf, apple slice, half a carrot or other such green tidbit. The doe will really appreciate it at this time. If you put it in the hutch she will be so intent upon it that you will be able to remove the nest box with little or no opposition. Take it out of her sight and carefully push the fur aside. If you can count the babies without picking them up, so much the better, but it's okay to put them aside and add up the tally.

Remove any dead ones, and if there are more than eight, you may want to foster the extras off to another doe who has fewer than eight, which is how many nipples a doe has. If there are any runts you may want to dispose of them, although I always let them live. Sometimes they will die in a few days but sometimes they will live and turn out just fine.

If you have bred two or more does at the same time, which is a good practice, you can foster young from a large litter to a doe with a smaller litter. If you have different colored rabbits, it's easy to record the color that gained a foster mom. If all are the same color, mark the ear of the transferred youngster with some ink from your tattoo kit. Just rub some on with your finger. It will remain for several weeks. Later you can rub on some more until it's time to tattoo a permanent number. You will want to keep track of fostered babies.

Most does won't mind accepting young from other mothers, and if the young are within a few days of the same age they will do nicely. But don't put in with older bunnies a brand new baby, because it will never survive in the fight for the nipple. If a doe is nervous, or you simply aren't sure whether she will accept another youngster, rub a little vanilla extract on her nose. This smell will linger long enough for the newcomer to pick up the scent of the rest of the litter and that's all it takes to gain social acceptance in the nest box.

EXTRA FEED FOR THE DOE

With the new litter looking for milk from the doe, it's a good idea to give her some extra feed. Of course, you will want her to have all the pellets she can eat. But in addition, she will appreciate a lettuce leaf or some other green tidbit each day. If you have a cow and extra milk, the doe and her growing litter will thrive if you can spare them some. Dried milk is good for the doe and so is Calf Manna. A tablespoon of Calf Manna daily will help the doe manufacture the milk her litter needs.

OUT COMES THE LITTER

In about 10 days the litter will open their eyes, and after three weeks they will come springing out of the box. Before they come out, I like to disinfect the hutch floor with a liquid germicide. In the meantime, I have kept a daily watch on the litter in the box, made sure that all the babies are together in one place in the nest, and have removed any that expired. The doe has been getting a green tidbit now and then, but when the litter pops out of the box, the greens cease.

IN GOES THE CREEP FEEDER;
OUT GOES THE NEST BOX

Quite often, creep feeding will boost the bunnies' growth, take some pressure off the doe, and allow you to breed her again sooner than you otherwise might. Creep feeders, available from rabbitry supply houses, let the bunnies eat a special high protein, milk replacer pellet, or even some whole oats, but prevent the doe from doing so. You don't want her getting too fat off some of the high-protein ration. The young will start nibbling away at the special creep feed as soon as they come out of the box, and you can let them keep eating it until they seem to prefer the regular pellets, or you can leave the creep feeder in until you wean them. It all depends upon how many of them there are, how much milk the doe has to offer, and whether you are going to wean them earlier than eight weeks. You may remove the nest box at 3-4 weeks of age.

BREEDING THE DOE AGAIN

For years normal practice was to wean the litter at eight weeks and breed the doe back at that time, thereby gaining a maximum of four litters per year per doe. But with advances in feeding, including regular pellets and also the creep feeding techniques, it is now possible to maintain the doe in good condition even if you breed her back earlier. Ordinarily, my practice is to rebreed the doe when the litter is four or five weeks old, and wean them at six or seven weeks. This gives her a week or two without the young to gain her strength for the next litter. And this gives me about five or six litters per year per doe. Some commercial breeders accelerate the breeding program to even seven or eight litters by rebreeding the doe sooner (and weaning the litter sooner).

Ordinarily, you will find it easier to get the doe to conceive if you breed her back while the litter is still running around in the hutch with her. If you give her a rest between litters she is apt to gain internal fat that will stop her from conceiving. It isn't necessary to wean the litter at eight weeks if you breed the doe again at that time; they may stay with her another couple of weeks. If she isn't bred back they may stay until they don't seem to be getting along anymore — usually about age three months. You may leave does with her almost interminably. Mothers and daughters get along just fine for months.

WEANING THE LITTER

Don't remove all the youngsters at the same time, because you want the doe to dry up gradually. Take out the biggest and huskiest of the youngsters; let the little ones stay in for some more milk. If you wean the litter over a period of about a week, the gradual process will be better for both mother and young. You may keep the litter in one hutch for another month (up to age three months) but after that time you will have to give each buck his own hutch, and it's a good idea to have a hutch for each young doe, although two to a hutch is good practice. If necessary, you can keep several does in one hutch, but each buck needs his own or battles will ensue.

Of course, if you are butchering or marketing meat rabbits at eight weeks or so, you may remove them directly from the mother's hutch and not concern yourself with growing pens. It's a good idea to have several smaller hutches, about two feet square for the medium and smaller breeds, for growing pens. Young bucks and does will do nicely in these, as you develop them for future breeding careers, for sale as breeders, or for show stock. If you like roaster-size eating rabbits you will need some hutches for them.

If you are raising medium size rabbits for meat, you will find it most economical to butcher or market them at eight weeks or so, because the weight they gain after this age is obtained on more pellets than the earlier poundage. Feed efficiency suffers, and so you will want to keep this in mind. Most processors want to buy rabbits at 4-5 pounds, so if you are supplying one of these you probably won't need to worry about a whole lot of developing pens. But it seems to me that at least a few will always be welcome. I never seem to have enough.

It is difficult to measure a rabbit's worth at eight weeks. If you are raising replacement or additional breeders, or show stock, you simply will have to develop them at least another month or so, depending upon the breed, before you can decide whether they should be kept or put into the pot. One reason that I like the smaller breeds is that they are still fryer-broiler size at three to four months of age. If I decide they are not worth keeping or selling as breeders, they still cook up very nicely — just like an eight-week-old medium breed fryer.

THE PROBLEMS OF WEATHER

What about breeding rabbits in the very hot or very cold months? Years ago, many rabbit breeders feared they would lose baby rabbits to hot weather, and some even constructed "cooling baskets" of wire screening in which they would place the babies during the warm days so that they would have plenty of ventilation. That was the era before the wire hutch and the wire nest box. Use of these two items of equipment makes the old cooling basket unnecessary and allows breeding right through the hottest part of summer.

The same equipment helps keep the litter warm in winter. Electric heating pads, encased in sheet metal, are made to fit the bottoms of the all-wire nest boxes, and may be purchased very economically. If they save one litter they pay for themselves.

Many other breeders take advantage of the open top of the wire hutch, provided it is under a roof, and place an aluminum photo reflector light over the nest box, with heat from a bulb radiating down through the top of the hutch. Others place such a light *under* the wire floor of the hutch below the nest box, and the litter burrows down into warmth. Such practices really are necessary only on the day or night of kindling, or perhaps for a day or two later in really cold weather. By that time the young begin to gain some fur and can stand the cold.

Winter or summer, ventilation is always necessary, and the wire hutch and the open box provide it. A wooden hutch may be too hot for summer. A closed nest box in winter can become damp. With today's equipment you can breed all year long.

BREEDING RECORDS

It can be seen from the preceding paragraphs that you simply must know when your does are bred. Otherwise, you'll never know when to install the nest box or expect the litter. This could lead to disaster. So you must record the dates and other information.

The doe's hutch card is the most important breeding record you can maintain. The illustration shows what is required in the doe's hutch card.

This card includes her birth date, name and ear identification number, and the names of her sire and dam. With this information you know when she's old enough to breed, and which buck to select for mating if you have more than one available.

When you mate the doe, you write in the name of the buck under "served by" and mark the date of service. If you remate her in a week or two while test-mating, you must record the additional date, but respect the first one, and give her the nest box the 27th day thereafter. If she does not kindle on time, you will remove the nest box but replace it 27 days after the second mating date. The rest of the blocks on the doe's hutch record card speak for themselves. Faithful use of them will reward you with valuable information that will help you decide how you will make further matings. The doe's hutch record card doubtless is the most important single record utilized in rabbit raising.

THE BUCK'S CARD

Also significant, however, is the buck's record card, particularly if you have a number of bucks in your rabbitry. The information entered in the boxes on the card will help you to evaluate the buck in the future. Both the doe and buck cards may be obtained free from feed dealers or by writing to feed companies, or you may prefer to draw up your own, perhaps including space for additional information that you find useful.

LITTER PRODUCTION RECORDS

Some breeders, particularly large commercial operators, maintain litter production records for all their bucks and does. I find this unnecessary for the backyard breeder who keeps hutch cards and refers to them regularly. I keep all the hutch cards needed over a course of a breeding career right on the hutch and do not need to transfer this information to other record sheets.

PEDIGREE AND
REGISTRATION CERTIFICATES

Another record useful in breeding is that of ancestry, and this is provided by pedigree and registration certificates. You will want to maintain pedigree records of all your rabbits. If you keep or sell a young rabbit for a breeder, it will need a pedigree certificate. You can easily write one out from the information contained on the pedigree or registration certificate of its sire and dam.

Still another handy record item, of particular use to the raiser who markets breeding stock, is the stock record book. This can be a composition book or looseleaf notebook. It contains a listing of all the rabbits in the herd (except for the unweaned bunnies). Entries are made for their breed, color, name, ear number, birth date, names and numbers of sire and dam, and any other information desired, such as weight at certain ages, or the quality of fur and markings. You may also want to enter the dates they were sold, and the names and addresses of the buyers. Keeping a list of customers helps in future selling. It helps too, to keep a carbon copy of all pedigrees of rabbits sold. They can help you supply a suitable rabbit in the future should your customer come back for more.

IDENTIFICATION BY TATTOOING

Every rabbit in your herd (above weaning age) should have a permanent ear number tattooed in its left ear. Not only do you need to number the rabbits for your own identification purposes, but the permanent number protects you from theft, brands the rabbit as one of yours when you sell it, and actually is required should you enter your rabbit in a show or have it registered in the ARBA registration system.

A starter tattoo set costs only a few dollars, and includes numbers zero through nine. In fact, a pen-type tattoo needle costs but a dollar or so. The latter type is more time-consuming to use, but works well if you have only a few rabbits to identify. Directions for use are simple: you merely prick the needle into the rabbit's left ear in a series of dots that represent a number. You may put in any number or letter you like, but put in a different one in each rabbit's ear. After the pricks are made, rub ink into the ear.

The plier type tattoo set takes less time to use. You merely insert the numbers (and letters) into the pliers, squeeze firmly and quickly on the rabbit's left ear, and then rub the tattoo ink into the ear, working it

Left: Plier-type tattooing kit. Right: In operation.

in well with a brush or your finger. You can wipe away the excess, or just let it dry and flake off.

As for identification numbers, as I said, you may use any letters and numbers you like. The tattoo pliers hold five letters or numbers. Some breeders put the rabbit's name in the ear, keeping it short, such as Kate, Jill or Jack. Others number them in sequence from number one. I put my initials, BB, in the ear, followed by three numbers that tell me which month the rabbit was born, how many were born so far that month, and the year. BB524, for example, was born in May, was the second rabbit marked in May, and the year was 1974. When I run out of numbers for rabbits born in the particular month, I start using letters. BB5A4 would be the 13th rabbit born in May of '74.

Use any system of coding that you find useful, but do mark each rabbit. Of course, you don't have to mark meat rabbits if you don't want to. Some breeders put the letters M-E-A-T or C-U-L-L in meat rabbits' ears, which would discourage another breeder from using them in a breeding program should they for some reason not find their way to the butcher. They naturally would be culls, or those not worth using for breeding.

WHY THE LEFT EAR?

The tattoo number goes into the left ear because the right is reserved for the registration number, which the rabbit may earn at maturity if it passes the registrar's examination.

The inked ear tattoo stands out clearly.

CHOOSING FUTURE BREEDERS

How do you decide which rabbits to keep for your breeding program, or for the shows, or to sell as breeders? Whole books have been written on the subject of animal breeding and genetics, and the principles apply to rabbits as well as other animals. If you would like to read more on this subject in detail, check the bibliography for recommended reading. In the meantime, we'll try to get you on the right track.

SELECTIVE BREEDING

There are several systems of breeding rabbits, but selection lies at the heart of all of them. Selection is the choosing, the selecting of those youngsters that you think will make the best future breeders. How well you choose will be the difference between being a rabbit breeder and a rabbit raiser. A breeder is one who does more than merely propagate the species. He does that, to be sure, but he does it in such a way that he maintains or improves high quality in his rabbits, so that they get better and better generation by generation.

WHAT IS 'BETTER'?

"Better" depends upon your goals. For the meat producer, better means more and better meat qualities. For the Angora raiser, it means more and longer hair. For the fancier, it means better body type, color, markings, etc.

But for all breeders, it means better health, better feed efficiency, larger litters and more.

Here are some general guidelines in selection. When you save youngsters for breeding, first of all make sure that you like the parents. The dam must be easy to breed. She must conceive consistently. She must have nice large litters. She must give plenty of milk. She must maintain perfect health.

The sire must be a good breeding buck and be of good body type, have good fur, be healthy, and sire large, healthy litters.

If you are raising meat rabbits, you want to save youngsters that have good shoulders, loins and rumps, gain rapidly and grow faster than their littermates. They should look as good as their parents, preferably better. The pair that produced them were good stock. You want to go uphill from there, so select future breeders from those that look and perform well.

WHAT ABOUT THE FANCIER?

The fancier, in addition to selecting for all the same factors as the meat producer, must also choose future breeders that he expects would score well against the point system carried in the standard for that breed. In the case of Tans, for example, color and markings make up much of the point scoring in the Tan standard. So in addition to being good healthy producers, Tans must have certain color factors and markings. The goal of the fancier is to produce a super rabbit, one that looks and performs superbly. That's why most rabbit raisers, no matter why they raise rabbits, look to the fancier for foundation stock.

The meat producer must also be something of a fancier because while he doesn't worry about markings, he certainly concerns himself with production goals and body type. He knows good blocky bucks and longer-bodied does will give him the good meaty fryer-broilers he wants to produce.

So in selection, you have to keep your goals in mind, and choose as future breeders those that come closest to meeting these goals. Don't expect to breed the perfect rabbit, but view each specimen as one half of a breeding team. For example, a weak-shouldered doe may be okay if you have a burly-shouldered buck. But don't choose two rabbits with the same failing, or you may breed in the weakness.

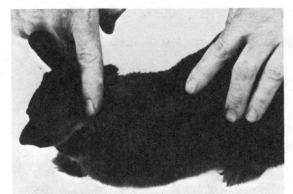

Fine and dense fur of the Tan springs back if it's stroked the wrong way.

A Tan is turned over to show the undercolor that gives the breed its name.

METHODS OF BREEDING

This brings us to the subject of breeding systems. Should you inbreed, linebreed, outcross or what? First of all, we had better define our terms.

Inbreeding is the breeding of close relatives, such as brother-sister, mother-son, cousins, etc. Linebreeding is a form of inbreeding that follows a line of descent, usually from an outstanding ancestor, and involves the use of relatives such as mother and grandson, aunt and nephew, grandsire and granddaughter, etc. Most successful rabbit breeders use a form of linebreeding. In other words, they inbreed on a line of direction and descent from an outstanding rabbit or rabbits they feel will maintain good quality and improve their stock.

Outcrossing is the use of an unrelated animal of the same breed in the breeding program. Most breeders resort to an outcross at one time or another, no matter how much they would like to keep it in the family. Crossbreeding is, of course, the mating of two different breeds.

Some successful breeders of meat rabbits have raised pure strains of New Zealand Whites and Californians and then made judicious crosses to provide a hybrid fryer. Some Angora wool producers have crossed varieties with good results. Generally speaking, however, crossing is better left to the experts or those of an experimental turn of mind.

For the past four years I have experimented with a cross between the Tan and the Netherland Dwarf, in an attempt to produce a Tan Dwarf, of which there are none to be found (although there is a standard for them). This effort has taken me through many generations, and I still am only getting close; there's a ways to go yet. So I can tell you that it is a time and hutch-consuming process with very little reward. And I'm only trying to produce a variety already written into the standard, not a new breed. There probably already are too many breeds of rabbits. Improvement of existing breeds is a worthy goal.

WHAT YOU HAVE PROBABLY HEARD ABOUT INBREEDING

Every example of human inbreeding you have ever seen has been a disaster. Marriage of close relatives is forbidden by law, but in our society we occasionally see the result of an incestuous relationship and we don't like it at all. In fact, we often see it in a side show. So how can inbreeding, the mating of close relatives, be any good for rabbits?

Well, inbreeding accentuates existing characteristics, both good and bad. If you breed two good animals, you can produce something better. If you breed two bad ones, the results can be worse. Those specimens in the side show are the result of a couple of mentally inferior parents — otherwise they wouldn't exist. The bad characteristics were accentuated.

YOU HAVE TO KNOW THE DIFFERENCE

Therefore, when breeding close rabbit relatives, you have to select only those that have the good characteristics you want in the offspring.

Every successful rabbit breeder I know practices inbreeding. And he inbreeds on a *line* of descent that will guarantee him a continuing parade of fine rabbits. But before he begins inbreeding on this line he (first) must have excellent foundation stock and (second) know clearly his breeding goals.

Inbreeding does not bring any new blood to a rabbitry, so maintenance of high quality and improvement will not take place for that reason. If a breeder did not have good foundation stock he would not get very far by inbreeding, but would be better off to introduce new blood. In fact, he would be better off to introduce 100 per cent new blood — get other rabbits.

But looking at inbreeding on a line from a practical standpoint, let's see what it can do for you. Let's assume you have begun with two pairs of rabbits from the same breeder, and which are at least distantly related.

WHERE TWO PAIRS CAN TAKE YOU

You breed the two pairs and two litters result. If you want to increase the size of the herd, you will want to breed the two pairs again, meanwhile saving offspring from the first two litters. If you save three does and two bucks from each litter, you might (1) breed a buck from one litter with a doe from the other (2) and (3) breed a doe from each litter back to her sire, (4) and (5) breed a doe from each litter to the other's sire, (6) breed a buck back to its dam and (7) breed the same buck to the other litter's dam. The possible results of this activity, over a period of several months, would be nine litters.

SELECTING FUTURE BREEDERS

These nine litters would provide a pool of breeding talent from which to *select* future breeders. We have already covered selection factors, but the way to select specific rabbits for future breeding is this: Each prospective new breeder should at least equal, preferably exceed, its sire and dam in selection qualities. Of course, each should be saved only from those parents already known to possess the desired characteristics, as determined by yourself or their former owner. And so it can be seen right here, if nowhere else, how important it is to begin with outstanding foundation stock, and why you should rely on the judgment of a respected breeder to start you right.

If in your breeding program you continue to select outstanding offspring from outstanding parents, consigning those that do not measure up directly to your pot, freezer or the friendly processor, you will be on your way to building a successful herd. At the same time you must choose, on a line of succession, those offspring and forebears to mate together. No two mates should possess the same weakness or the resultant litter will possess a double "dose" of that weakness and will be a disappointment.

But if you have selected wisely, the litter will receive a double dose of good qualities and only a single dose of a weakness and you will be delighted with the litter. Of course, some individuals will be "better" than others. It is up to you to recognize what "better" is and ingrain it into your herd by breeding together those "better" animals. This ability will be gained by study of your animals, the standard, and by keeping in mind your breeding goals. Examination by a registrar and comparison of your animals by a judge certainly will help. But the biggest responsibility lies with you, because most of the really important qualities of your stock will be found only in the breeding hutches and the nest boxes.

OUTCROSSING

If all your best efforts at linebreeding fail to produce the desired results, perhaps because your foundation stock was not all it should have been; or, if your first attempts at selection took your stock down hill instead of upgrade, you may want to resort to an outcross, within your breed and variety, of course. Almost every breeder does so at one time or another. I have used imported animals in hopes of improving my own when a characteristic mine lacked was found abroad. As a rule, however, it is wise to avoid outcrossing if possible, because the introduction of new genes can confuse the situation more than help it. You can't be as sure of what you will get (unless you are familiar with the forebears of the foreign or unrelated rabbit).

Start with the best possible foundation stock. Mate the best offspring back to the best parents and inbreed this way on a line of descent from the best. Resort to an outcross sparingly. Remember that the offspring are proof of the parents' ability to produce; keep breeding only those parents who produce the kind of young you want. This might take a few litters to determine.

Improvement is a slow process, but it is steady if you follow the rules of good sense and read up on genetics. The perfect rabbit has not been bred. It never will be, because whenever anyone gets close, the standard is rewritten to make perfection just a little better. And what a pity if we were able to achieve perfection, for all the fun of pursuit of it would disappear.

7
Selling Rabbits
The Modern Way

If you start raising rabbits right you doubtless will sell some whether you really want to or not. You'll have nice rabbits and people will want to buy them. They will wave the money at you and you will, if you are like most of us, take it.

They will want your rabbits for meat, laboratory use, breeding stock or pets. And even if you have only a very few breeders and a voracious appetite for rabbit, you probably will have some extra rabbits to sell. Should you raise a lot of rabbits, you will be looking to sell some.

Of course, success in selling rabbits depends upon, as pointed out earlier, choice of a breed for which you have a market. Let's look at some of these markets:

MEAT

The easiest way to sell meat rabbits is to sell them live to a processor. Some processors pick them up at your rabbitry. Others want you to deliver. Either way, you have to talk to the processor to see how many and what size rabbits he wants, and when he wants them. You can locate a processor by talking to other breeders in your area. You can see them at a local club meeting, which is just one of the benefits of club membership that we will discuss in Chapter 11.

While selling live to a processor is the easiest way, it is not necessarily the most lucrative, particularly for the small raiser. The price you receive will be the lowest possible return you can get for your rabbits. It will pay you to sell live meat rabbits to a processor only if you have neither the time nor the inclination to make a greater effort with a correspondingly greater return.

You may, for example, be able to gain a better price by selling live to a meat market which will also do the butchering and thus cut out the processor's profit. He will be able to make a greater margin and pay you a little more. The same may be true of a restaurant or an institution, such as a hospital or a school.

You may be able to develop a list of customers who will buy rabbits live to butcher for their own table. Many rabbit raisers have acquired a waiting market just by starting with live sales to friends, relatives, neighbors and co-workers.

These are people who will pay you a little more than will the processor, but will still be getting meat for their table at the lowest possible price short of raising rabbits themselves.

DRESSED MEAT

If you have only a few rabbits to sell for meat, or a lot of spare time, you will find more profit in selling dressed rabbit meat. You will have to meet local requirements for butchering, which will require knowledge of Health Department regulations. Butchering is not difficult but must be done under sanitary conditions.

You may develop a list of customers for dressed rabbit meat among relatives, friends, neighbors and co-workers, restaurants, stores and institutions. For this market, you may expect a return much greater than you can receive for live meat sales, but of course you must have the proper facilities, including freezer space.

Home butchering for your own family's consumption is a simple procedure and may be carried out in the garage or basement. Rabbit meat can be packaged in styrofoam trays with plastic wrap, or in cartons supplied at a nominal charge by feed companies. Or, you may simply wrap them in freezer paper.

Killing and dressing a rabbit is relatively simple. Hold the rabbit by the hind feet and quickly snap its head down and back, breaking the neck and killing it. Cut off the head and hang it upside down by the hind feet and let it bleed. A couple of nails in a board hung on the wall will hold it. I like to hang a plastic garbage bag on the nails, with the rabbit hanging above the bag. Cut the skin around each hock and slit from hock to anus inside each leg. Then you simply pull the skin down over the carcass as you'd peel off a pullover sweater. Put the pelt aside for the moment and slit the carcass from tail to abdomen, cutting around the anal opening between the hind legs. Save the heart, kidneys and liver but let the rest of the entrails fall into the plastic bag for disposal.

Simple method of killing a rabbit with a quick snap of its neck.

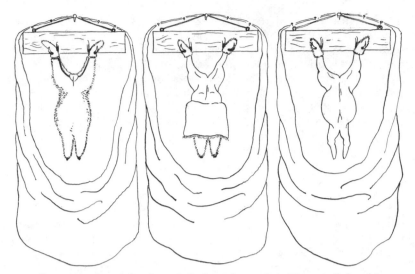

Cut around each hock and slit from leg to leg. Then pull the skin down over the carcass the way you would peel off a pullover sweater.

On a cutting board, split the hind legs from the back. Cut the back into two or three pieces, depending upon the size of the rabbit. Cut the forelegs apart and wash all the pieces under running water, removing any hair that might have clung to them. I like to chill the pieces in the refrigerator before my wife wraps and freezes the rabbit. I don't sell any dressed rabbit meat so I don't bother with fancy packaging that you would want to consider if you were offering the meat for sale.

MEAT PRICES

Here's a rundown of current average price ranges for meat rabbits in my area. These prices fluctuate as do all meat prices and are tied pretty closely to the cost of feed, which currently is just beginning to slip from an all-time high.

Received from a middle man who picks up live and delivers to a processor: 50 cents a pound.

From a processor, who buys live what I deliver: 60 cents a pound.

From a restaurant, who buys live what I deliver: 70 cents a pound.

From friends, restaurants, stores, dressed and packaged: $1.25 to $1.75 per pound.

With feed costs running $8 to $10 per hundredweight and figuring a feed conversion ratio of 4:1 (four pounds of feed to one pound live weight), it costs 32 to 40 cents to produce a pound of live weight. With dressout at about 50 per cent of live weight (you may do better — up to 60 per cent), your income over feed costs for a four-pound liveweight fryer amounts to 10-18 cents per pound from the middleman, another dime from the processor, another dime from the restaurant, and a much better return for the dressed meat. The last can bring you an income over feed cost of more than $1 per pound, but there is additional investment required in butchering facilities and equipment.

The margin in live sales is small, requiring a large volume. Dressed meat sales are better, but if you produce only a few rabbits and like the way they taste, you may want to put them in your own freezer, as I do, and take the savings on the grocery bill.

An additional source of income in dressed meat sales, or rabbits for home consumption, is the pelt. This pelt should be dried on a spring wire shaper, with the fat first scraped from it. Several pelts, once dry, store nicely in a plastic bag, with moth balls. You may have them tanned, tan them yourself, or simply sell them dried. Current prices paid for dried pelts are about 25 cents each, so every four is another dollar. It will cost you about 40 cents to have them tanned, or you may tan them yourself and receive a dollar or two for them, or you may wish to make them into articles to sell. Perhaps you can locate a store that sells novelties and would like to carry some of the tanned pelts. You might know someone who makes stuffed animals and pillows. You or another member of your family might try this yourself.

I have never tanned a rabbit skin because it looks like a time-consuming job and so I'm not going to recommend that you try it. I should add here that I get my pelts tanned for free by giving half of all my pelts to a friend who sends them away to be tanned. I wind up with only half the pelts, but they are tanned for free.

Scraped pelt is dried on a wire stretcher. Then it may be sold or tanned, to use the fur to make articles such as this little girl's warm and soft fur muff and hat set.

The best instructions for tanning are contained in the book *Tan Your Hide!* by Phyllis Hobson. This is a 144-page paperback book that includes correct skinning methods, stretching and curing fur skins, storing and shipping, tools and methods for tanning, materials, formulas, and special patterns for making garments at home from your skins. It may be obtained from your bookstore, or may be ordered directly from Garden Way Publishing. See page 146 for more information.

LABORATORY SALES

Obtaining a contract for direct sales to a laboratory is not the easiest thing a new raiser can do. He must meet strict standards of management and sanitation, but that's not the hard part. If you follow housing and equipment instructions in this book you will be able to obtain certification to produce laboratory rabbits. What's difficult is being able to supply the number of laboratory rabbits that may be needed. The way most breeders start out therefore, is to sell to a middleman, who ordinarily is a larger breeder who supplements his own laboratory stock production by buying from others. You may contact hospitals and pharmaceutical companies in your area, along with universities, to obtain information about their requirements for laboratory stock. They may tell you they are already obtaining lab stock from someone else. If so, ask his name and contact him. He may need a supplemental supply. Another way to find out who is buying lab rabbits (and all other kinds) is through your local rabbit breeders association. There is more information about them in Chapter 11.

BREEDING STOCK SALES

Sales of breeding stock will bring the greatest return to your rabbitry, and you should try to sell some breeding stock — the best of your meat or lab production that is surplus to your own breeding requirements. This is the most difficult, but the most lucrative way to dispose of your rabbits.

When selling breeding stock, try to have at least two litters of young available at all times, because few people want to start breeding from a brother and sister pair. It's always a good idea to breed two does at the same time anyway, and if you do you will always have at least two litters from which to sell breeding stock.

As you gain experience with your breed, you will be able to tell at fryer marketing time (about eight weeks for the medium breeds) which rabbits are better than others. Hold these back from the meat market for prospective breeders. By age three months, for most breeds, you will be able to tell if they are in fact good potential breeding stock. I wouldn't sell any rabbits for breeding under this age except in the case of some marked breeds, such as Dutch, whose value lies in color and markings to a greater extent than others. These characteristics are apparent at an early age.

But for most breeds, you really can't make a valid judgment until they are at least three months old, so you will want to retain the young at least until that age. Does may be kept together almost until breeding age, but the bucks should be given separate cages at about three months because otherwise they will begin to fight. Actually, this will not entail a great many hutches because you will not need to retain as many bucks as does. Not only is there a greater demand for does initially, but the recurring need is greater because they have a shorter breeding career than the bucks. Does will bear litters for about three years; bucks will sire them two to three times as long.

ADVERTISING YOUR BREEDING STOCK

While a ready market awaits your meat and laboratory production, you must create a breeding stock market. One of the best ways to do this is by advertising.

The classified pages of your local newspaper will work hard for you. A small town daily or a weekly paper is usually better than a large daily.

Throughout the country there are a number of classified ad newsletters that are published locally or regionally and charge only a percentage of sales as a commission. One in my area charges 10 per cent, which is typical, and only after the sale is made. I am able to advertise at no cost unless I sell. And I build the price of the ad, the commission, into my selling price.

The local feed store, where you purchase your rabbit pellets, usually has a bulletin board where you may advertise your rabbits. A 3x5 file card, or a business card tacked on the board will bring you customers.

National advertising in magazines will also bring customers. Resort to national advertising only when you have a supply large and steady enough to make it pay. Don't advertise nationally if you have only a dozen or so rabbits to sell. Not only will they hardly pay for the ad, they may already be sold locally by the time the ad appears in the magazine.

SMALL AND STEADY

Regardless of where you advertise, you will get your best results from small but frequent advertisements. Be a steady advertiser. Be known as someone who always has rabbits for sale — all year. And be the steady producer who can keep on advertising. If you have a steady supply and advertise steadily, you will find a continuing demand for your stock.

If you advertise locally, such as in the classified pages, don't give out much information over the phone. Don't give prices — only a range of prices if you are pushed. Try to get the caller to come and see your rabbits. If they are nice rabbits they will do the selling for you. If you give prices over the phone you may regret it. People are funny. If you tell them that a rabbit costs $10, some will think it's too much and some will think it's too little. When Netherland Dwarfs were selling at about $50 each a few years ago when they made their debut on these shores, a friend of mine tried to sell some for $25 but had little success until he raised his prices. Buyers wanted to pay more because they felt they were purchasing a high class item.

WHEN THE PHONE RINGS

When you receive a telephone call as a result of your local advertising, tell the caller the name of the breed or breeds you have. Explain that they are very nice rabbits, pedigreed, kept under the best of conditions, and are the offspring of champions (if such is the case). Say that they are reasonably priced and that the buyer should really come and look them over and that you would be delighted to show them — perhaps next weekend.

LETTERS OF INQUIRY

Your national advertising will bring more letters than phone calls. You will find it helpful to answer these with a mimeographed letter of information that describes what you have to offer, such as the one I use, as follows:

Bob Bennett
One Governor's Lane
Shelburne, Vermont 05482

Dear

I breed and exhibit pedigreed Tans in all four colors: Chocolate, Lilac, Black and Blue.

These are from the best bloodlines in the United States, England and Europe. Years ago when I started with Tans, I spared no expense in obtaining foundation stock. I keep my breeders ARBA Registered. Several are Grand Champions. They produce top winners in national shows every year. Ask anyone who has Tans about mine. They know about them. That's one reason why they are My Famous Tans.

All the stock I sell is guaranteed to satisfy or your purchase price refunded and shipping arrangements made. I supply full, detailed pedigree papers.

My Tans are kept in all-wire hutches with hopper feeders and heated, piped, drinker valve-dispensed water. I utilize the most modern management tools and techniques. I stress nutrition, sanitation and preventive medicine.

Unless other arrangements are made, I ship in lightweight disposable crates by Air Express, shipping charges collect. I can estimate charges in advance if you desire.

I drive the rabbits myself to specific flights at Burlington International Airport. I can ship any time of year. In most cases you can pick up your stock at your airport only hours after it leaves my hutches — even if you live in California. The rabbits are in transit less time than they are to travel to the average show.

Should you desire to place an order, send a money order or check, along with your telephone number and the name of the airport where stock should be sent. I recommend you pick up stock at your airport if possible, but it can be delivered by truck to your door if you wish. I will notify you when to expect your Tans.

I have found it advantageous to enclose this form letter because of the volume of my mail. But be assured I am ready to answer any questions you may have.

Thank you very much for your interest in My Famous Tans. I hope to be able to serve you. My wish is that you will obtain the same enjoyment from my rabbits as I do.

Sincerely,

If you insert an ad into *Domestic Rabbits* magazine, which is the best medium for reaching rabbit raisers in the United States, its possessions, Canada, and even some foreign countries, you will want to have a good supply of these mimeographed letters, because your ad will bring many inquiries. In addition, you may find it useful to reply with a carbon set speed letter. With a speed letter, you can give information about specific stock available, and prices (you must of course give prices in the mail), and answers to questions.

When I receive an inquiry, I reply with the mimeographed letter, the speed letter and a stamped, self-addressed envelope in which the prospective customer replies with his copy of the speed letter. I find that his system brings more sales than any other.

ADDITIONAL CORRESPONDENCE

You may find yourself answering lots of questions about your rabbits and it may take you several letters before a prospect decides to buy, so allow plenty of stamps and time for correspondence. That's all part of selling breeding stock by mail.

Of course, you can't send the rabbits in a letter. So, after you have received an order, ship by Air Express. You will have to check the Air Express office at your airport for crating regulations, as these seem to vary all over the country. But you can easily ship rabbits by Air Express anywhere in the world. Depending upon express office regulations, you can ship "charges collect" to the purchaser. Of all the many hundreds of rabbits I have shipped over the years, only one has died in transit that I know of, and it was insured so the express company absorbed the loss.

When you ship by air to a distant purchaser, you are the one who is picking out the rabbits, not the buyer. And that is the way it always should be, because you will know better which two rabbits will make the best pair. And so it is no handicap to the buyer to be unable to visit the rabbitry. And you might also prefer the mail order aspect of the rabbit business, because it lets you conduct it on your time, at your convenience. Such is not always the case when you entertain visitors to your rabbitry.

You may also sell rabbits at shows, but your best bet will be delivery, not sales. In other words, by correspondence you should make the sale, and deliver at the show out of convenience to yourself and the buyer, to save delivery charges. If you are a winner at shows, you will find you will receive lots of inquiries. And you may wish to take pairs, trios or quartets or more of rabbits for sale. Make sure that you select those for sale; don't get into the habit of selling winners simply because a particular judge liked them that day.

It may pay you to purchase ads in the show catalogs, stating you will deliver to the show. Take orders in the mail or over the phone.

THE IRON-CLAD GUARANTEE

You want satisfied customers. And the best way to find customers who return is to sell them rabbits that won't. In other words, you must sell good rabbits to get repeat orders. Don't sell anybody a rabbit you wouldn't like to have yourself. Of course, this is easier said than done sometimes. Once in a while you will find a customer who is unhappy. It happens to everyone who sells anything.

I find that the best guarantee that can be made is one of my best sales tools. If you sell a meat, laboratory or breeding rabbit, guarantee absolute satisfaction or money back or another rabbit, at the option of the buyer. Meat and laboratory business is built upon repeat orders, and the iron-clad guarantee for these sales is mandatory. But it is just as necessary in breeding stock sales. Even if the purchaser doesn't buy any more from you, you want his good will and good recommendation to others. And so, make the guarantee I make. Absolute satisfaction or money back or another rabbit, whichever makes him happy. This means no quibbling. If he doesn't like the rabbit for any reason, even a stupid one, do right by him. Give him his money or another rabbit.

BUT FOR HOW LONG?

Fine, you say, but suppose the rabbit dies of old age and he wants another 10 years later. Well, that's ridiculous. And, of course, if he doesn't take care of the rabbit and it dies a few months later, certainly you have no responsibility. But I have replaced rabbits that died even a year later, simply to make a friend. Is this good business? You bet it is. If I have a hundred rabbits, and a customer who bought four loses one, it doesn't hurt me a bit to give him another. In fact, it does a world of good. The customer often buys more, becomes a friend and one of my best salesmen, because he tells his friends he was treated right.

GOOD RECORDS MAKE FUTURE SALES

When you sell a rabbit, keep a record of the name and address of the purchaser. If you give a pedigree with the animal, keep a carbon copy. Whenever you get overstocked, or have some rabbits you think he might like for some reason or another, drop him a postcard. In fact, a good way to make sales is to mimeograph a postcard sales pitch and send it off to all your customers and to those who have inquired about your rabbits in the past. Another way to make sales through the mail is to look up names of new members of the ARBA who live within driving distance and to invite them to your rabbitry. Each year I pay for the cost of my ARBA membership with a postcard. I always look up the new members listed in the Yearbook and send them a card. I have yet to miss selling to at least one of these prospects each year. I can give you lots of reasons for joining the ARBA, but this ought to sell you on the idea if nothing else does.

What's the best way to sell rabbits — regardless of their end use of meat, laboratory or breeding stock? Have them for sale. That may sound silly, because if you don't have any, you can't sell them. But if you do, and regularly, and the right kind, you will become known as a steady source of supply. And that's what will make most of your sales for you.

WHAT ELSE TO SELL?

You can sell meat, laboratory and breeding stock, and even pets, if you must. You can sell pelts and, if you have Angoras, you can sell wool. What else can you sell?

FIRST, EQUIPMENT

If you build all-wire cages like those in this book, you will find they are simple to construct and that you can do it in very little time after you have built a few. Many rabbit raisers build and sell these cages and derive as much income from them as they do from their rabbits. I'm among them. I build scores of these hutches each year, offering them for sale with breeding rabbits. But I also put them into pet stores on consignment, and quite a few are sold there. I'm opposed to the sale of pet rabbits, but inasmuch as thousands are sold, I feel they should have good housing and so I'm glad to be able to offer these hutches to the owners of pet rabbits.

You may also purchase large quantities of other equipment, such as watering and feeding supplies, nest boxes, etc., at a discount, and sell them at a unit price that allows a profit and yet is attractive to the local purchaser. In many areas, rabbitry equipment is not available locally and there is a good opportunity to carry such a line. As your volume builds, you may become a distributor or dealer and qualify for wholesale prices.

For those who want to build their own hutches, you may provide the wire and the various hardware and tools, which, again, you can buy in quantity.

MANURE FOR THE ROSE GARDENERS

Rabbits can return you so much in so many ways. The local rose gardeners flock to a nearby garden supply center which stocks manure from my rabbitry. The price is preposterous, but the demand is brisk. As more and more people become interested in gardening, and as the supply of other animal manures becomes smaller, the demand for rabbit manure increases. Rabbit manure does not burn and so it can be applied directly. In the next chapter I'll explain how I use it in my own garden and for the flowers, shrubbery and even the lawn. But for the local garden center, you may want to do as I do and bag the manure in empty feed sacks, and let the rose gardeners and others pay dearly for it. I have calculated that every three bags of manure I sell wholesale buys one bag of feed. And I could pay for a lot more of my feed bill with this manure if I didn't want to use so much of it myself.

WORMS FOR THE FISHERMAN

Under the manure that lies beneath my wire hutches wriggles a nice pocketful of spending money for my two sons. Fishworms bring 25 cents a dozen wholesale in these parts, and it is no trouble for a couple of young boys to unload 100 dozen a week during the spring and summer to a couple of sporting goods stores that supply the cardboard containers free. All they have to do is fork over the manure and pick up the money. Fishermen aren't simply a lazy bunch. It's just that fewer and fewer of them want to dig holes in their lawns these days, and even if they did they would find few worms. Chemical fertilizers have chased a lot of them away.

There are several books available on worm culture. I have read a couple of them. I suppose I could produce more worms if I followed the authors' tips. But I find that beneath the hutches, and inside my compost heaps are all the worms anybody could want, without making any additional effort. I didn't plant them there, they simply arrived. Selling them is a source of income you might not have anticipated. In the next two chapters I'll explain two other ways they help you with your rabbits.

8
Rabbits And
The Home Garden

Rabbits can help your garden produce more, and your garden can do the same for your rabbits. The manure is great for growing most anything, and some garden produce, in spite of what I told you in the chapter on feeding, can help you grow your rabbits.

Rabbit manure contains higher proportions of nitrogen and phosphorous than other manures, and more potash than most. It will not burn plants even when applied fresh. It comes in a convenient round, dry form. I can't get enough of the stuff and everybdy keeps trying to buy it from me.

MAKE IT GO A LONG WAY

You can use rabbit manure just the way it is, forked up from under the hutches. But composting it with other materials will make it go further and enhance its value as an all-around fertilizer.

Twice a year I push wheelbarrows full of manure to a wooded area in the back of my property and build compost heaps. In November, when all the leaves fall from my large oak trees, I build piles of alternating layers of rabbit manure and leaves, with intermittent sprinklings of superphosphate, lime, and sometimes some chemical fertilizer. In the springtime I build additional heaps using more manure and leftover leaves plus those that are found in the spring cleanup. Later I add grass clippings to the heaps and thus I have a supply of late summer compost to follow my spring output.

Follow any good composting scheme, add rabbit manure and watch things grow. If it doesn't rot fast enough for me, I get out my shredder and grind it all up.

WHERE AND HOW TO USE IT

Rabbit manure compost can be dug and tilled into any garden with good results. It improves the texture of the soil, making it more receptive to rain and generally improving the flowers or vegetables. I add lime to the oak leaf manure compost for most uses, but around the azaleas and rhododendrons, which like an acid soil environment, I leave it out. Usually one of my compost heaps is an acid one, while the other is sweetened with lime.

If you dig the compost in before planting time, you'll soon have a good stand of whatever it is you are growing. That's the time to mulch with more compost. For my flower beds, I shred the compost fine and mulch the beds quite neatly. The mulch conserves moisture, smothers weeds, and keeps the beds attractive and care free. The following spring I dig in this mulch with some additional compost and start all over. I don't see how you can put in too much rabbit manure compost.

Into the vegetable garden goes wheelbarrow after wheelbarrow of compost before rototilling in the spring. Into each planting row goes some finely shredded compost. Into each hill of vine crops, such as cucumbers, squash, pumpkins and melons, goes a bushel basket full of compost. Vine crops really thrive on the stuff. When everything is up and growing, I don't have to hoe weeds. I smother them and conserve moisture by banking a compost mulch around every row and hill. Next spring, just as in the flower garden, this mulch is tilled under and the whole process starts again.

RABBIT MANURE
SAVES ENERGY, TOO!

In days of old, before heating cables, hot beds often were heated with stable manure. A few years ago I found an old gardening book with directions, and substituted rabbit manure for the horse variety. Now I start my tomato and pepper plants and my impatiens annual flowers in a rabbit manure hot bed made of old storm windows into which goes about a two-foot depth of droppings. In late February here in New Jersey I start the hot bed and by Mother's Day I've got hundreds of vegetable and flower plants. Electricity bill: $00.00. The true test of the capability of rabbit manure to heat a hot bed when the temperature is way below freezing outside is the impatiens. This annual flower seed, which I save from year to year for plenty of color in the shade, takes about three weeks to germinate. The sustaining bottom heat of the rabbit manure does the job.

HELP FROM THE WORM

Fat, wriggly red worms inhabit the compost heap, partly because they are attracted to it and find it a comfortable and palatable environment, and partly because I put them there with the manure when I clean out my rabbit shed. These worms do a great job of converting the manure into good rich black potting soil. For starting seeds I know nothing better. Down at the bottom of the compost heap you'll find good potting soil just for the digging.

WHAT ABOUT THE LAWN?

Rabbit manure and rabbit manure compost can also go on the lawn as a top dressing at any time of the year, but a little caution should be taken. If you feed pellets or re-cleaned grains, the manure will not contain weed seeds. But if you add hay and straw, you might not like the looks of your lawn if you use rabbit manure.

I use a chemical fertilizer on my front lawn and the rabbit manure in the back. I get some weeds with the rabbit manure, but I don't mind them so much in the back where part of the lawn is worn away for a pitcher's mound and home plate and a sand box and a gym set. A spray weed killer gets rid of some weeds, too.

For the lawn, either I run the compost through my shredder to make it fine enough for my fertilizer spreader to handle, or I sift it through a frame of two by fours and hardware cloth. You don't want it so coarse it will mat and smother the lawn. It must be fine enough to let the blades of grass through. A friend of mine spreads this compost and straight dried rabbit manure on his yard all winter long. He's the first one in town to crank up the lawnmower in the spring.

COMPOSTED AND DRY

Rabbit manure will not create any odor problems for you if you keep it dry and composted. If it sits in a pit, soaking with urine, you'll have trouble handling it. Well-drained, graveled beds under the hutches will keep it dry.

WHAT THE GARDEN CAN DO
FOR THE RABBITS

I insisted in Chapter 5 that you feed rabbit pellets. And I stand on those statements. But the garden can supplement the pellets by providing root, green, grain and seed crops that you'll find useful as you progress in rabbit raising. Some of them are particularly useful for kindling does and show stock. I don't suggest that anyone try to feed rabbits exclusively on the output of a garden. But since my rabbits put so much into my garden, I figure they deserve to get something out of it.

Sunflower seeds are an excellent fur conditioner. All rabbits love them, but they are especially good for those you plan to show. And sunflowers are a cinch to grow at the back of the garden, perhaps among the corn, where they won't shade lower-growing vegetables.

Corn is great for rabbits. Corn is also great for humans, so perhaps there won't be any left for the stock. But rabbits like the dried corn stalks and shucks and, if you can spare them, a few ears. After they have dried, they will soon devour them, cob and all. A few green shucks won't hurt, either, provided you don't give them too many.

Pumpkin seeds are eaten by some rabbits, snubbed by others. We always grow some big jack o'lantern pumpkins and we dry the seeds for the rabbits.

Mangel beets have been grown for years and years in Europe as a stock feed. These are huge beets which I leave in the ground and cover with leaves into late fall and winter. Then I slice them for the rabbits. A number of years ago I had a nicely marked Dutch buck that never seemed to put on enough weight to win in a show. He did as poorly as 11th in a class of 11. I lent him to a friend one fall and by the time I got him back in the spring he was so plump he won best of breed out of 77 Dutch rabbits. Mangels did the trick over the winter and since then I have fed them to rabbits who need to put on a little weight and don't seem to do it otherwise. You may have to check the seed catalogs closely to find mangel seeds, but they are available. I get mine from Burpee.

Rutabagas are those big turnips. I grow these with the mangels and leave them in the ground, too. Whenever I need them I just dig them out. I feed these to adult rabbits that like them better than mangels. Rabbits are individuals and have their individual tastes.

Nobody likes turnips in my family except the rabbits and me. I eat most of them, but there are always some roots left over. Again, these are left covered in the ground in late fall and winter.

If rabbits will eat anything, they'll eat carrots. The problem is that the humans want them too. I usually snitch a few and feed them to newly kindled does and my favorite old bucks. I dry the tops like hay and feed them to one and all. When I thin the young carrots I dry the whole business and feed to all.

Lettuce thinnings are also dried for all or fed green to adults very sparingly. A new mother will always get some lettuce.

I have dried bean and pea vines like hay and fed them to all.

If you have the room, grow your own alfalfa, clover hay and even soybeans. Can you grow oats? If so, you've got grain and straw.

The thing to remember is that these feeds are merely supplements.

If you want to put meat on your rabbits, if you want top flesh condition, you must feed pellets. Grains, greens and roots are treats in addition to the pellets — don't try to make them do too much.

The home garden isn't the only place these and other feeds are found. You can get your vegetable store to save you the tops and the castoffs — but be sure to wash them well. Feeds pop up in other places. One friend of mine lives near a huge bakery. When the freight cars roll in to unload the wheat some spillage occurs. He scoops up 50 pounds of whole wheat a week and uses it to supplement the pellet ration.

Dandelions, plantains, dry bread, leftover cereal (with milk!) — these are other feeds that can supplement the pellets and are better fed than wasted, particularly to non-productive animals who may be lazing along through the summer. These feeds won't do much for great production, but are helpful for maintenance.

Remember that young rabbits can't handle green feeds — it may give them diarrhea.

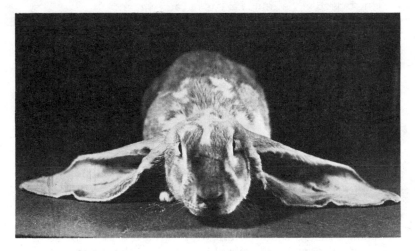

A handsome English Lop

9
Problems

Good routine management and preventive measures will help you keep your rabbits productive and healthy, your rabbitry attractive and sweet smelling. Such practice will minimize four basic types of problems in rabbit raising: breeding, disease, poor sanitation and unattractiveness. The first can prevent you from even starting in rabbit production; the last can incite a zoning board to put you out of business.

BREEDING TIPS

First let's look at breeding problems. Here are a few guidelines practiced by many successful breeders:

Keep bucks and does in good flesh and fur condition. Don't let those does get too fat.

Mate your does on weekends at six-to-eight-hour intervals. You may then expect litters on Tuesdays and Wednesdays. This means that you'll have time on the previous weekends to prepare nest boxes. If there are children in the neighborhood, they will be in school in midweek when litters are kindled, making for a quiet birthday. Keep a close eye on hutch cards and calendars.

Always check vulvas for that reddish purple color that means does are ready for service. Always check testicles to make sure they are fat and full, indicating virility.

Test-mate your does a week later, and learn which does test-mate positively (see earlier, Chapter 6). Learn to palpate does (see also Chapter 6).

Try not to handle does three weeks after mating. And don't allow visitors into the rabbitry when does are due to kindle. Keep things nice and quiet at kindling time.

The day after kindling, distract the doe with a green tidbit before inspecting the litter.

Use extra insulation and nesting material in cold-weather nest boxes. Provide heat with a light or nest box heater.

Use a well-ventilated nest box in hot weather. The type made of cage floor wire works well.

If you should lose a litter, rebreed the doe within a couple of days. If she kills her litter give her a second chance. If you want, give her a third chance. But three times and she's out.

Never mate two rabbits with the same fault, e.g., poor fur or body type.

PREVENTING DISEASE

Of course, always start with healthy stock which exhibits a bright eye, glossy coat, firm flesh and vigor. Isolate all new stock away from the herd for a week before introducing into the rabbitry. A pen in the garage, tool shed or near the garden may be necessary.

Maintain a good feeding schedule of the proper feeds. Never give greens to very young rabbits.

Keep the water fresh and pure. If you have crocks, rinse daily, wash and disinfect weekly. If you use an automatic, piped system, observe valves daily and flush the system regularly.

If rabbits aren't eating, something's wrong. First make sure they are getting enough water. Rabbits without water won't eat.

Check for that bright eye, glossy coat; feel for the firm flesh and observe activity. Keep a close watch on your stock.

Check footpads occasionally to avoid sore hocks. If one rabbit is a habitual stomper, put a flat board in the hutch for him to stomp.

Watch the droppings. They should be large, round and firm. Take action at the first sight of any diarrhea.

Watch for runny noses indicating colds. Keep an ear out for sneezes. Matted fur on the insides of front paws means rabbits have been wiping runny noses.

Don't be afraid to dispose of diseased stock. If you have rabbits with colds or pneumonia it may cost you far more to cure them than to replace them. And I don't mean the cost of medicine or even the vet's fee. They may bequeath their poor health to offspring and generate a whole herd of health problems. Most disease problems — and there really are few that hit rabbits hard — can be prevented. Some can be treated successfully. But some aren't worth fooling around with. A swift blow on the skull can be a foolproof cure.

ROUTINE PREVENTIVE MEDICINE

The main thing to keep in mind with herd health is to maintain it, not recapture it. Recovered rabbits often don't ever measure up to those that have always enjoyed perfect health. They don't grow or mature as they should. And they often aren't worth the time it takes to treat. So prevent disease problems by following a good routine of preventive medicine.

Here's the routine I follow — one that has kept my closely quartered stock in good health for years.

One week a month I treat the water with a sulfaquinoxaline sodium solution. This helps prevent coccidiosis and diarrhea.

Once a week I treat the water with Terramycin or Neo-Terramycin Soluble Powder for growth promotion, diarrhea prevention, and because I'm absolutely certain it increases litter size.

Before each litter emerges from the nest box at two-to-three weeks of age, I disinfect the hutch floor.

When the litter reaches four weeks of age I provide a crock of water treated with Emtryl soluble powder as the only source of water to prevent mucoid enteritis. I continue this for two weeks.

This may sound like some trouble and expense. But I can assure you that these measures are cheap and trouble-free if you look at the health record my stock has maintained:

Very little diarrhea. No sign of coccidiosis. Not a sniffle in five years! Drastic reduction of mortality of young stock due to mucoid or non-specific enteritis. Practically no mortality of mature stock. Larger average litter size than anyone else who raises my particular breed.

Let's take a closer look at this preventive medicine — the *best* medicine.

Sulfaquinoxaline sodium helps prevent coccidiosis or spotted liver. Packers of rabbit meat have found liver coccidiosis quite prevalent in rabbits. Packers must discard the liver — and some won't buy more rabbits from producers whose rabbits exhibit the spotted liver. Infected rabbits are not thrifty and fail to gain weight properly. They are also more susceptible to other intestinal problems. Sulfaquinoxaline sodium is sold in all feed and farm supply stores, but you should get yours from a rabbitry supply house, which will provide the instructions you need for use in your rabbitry. These vary with different concentrations and forms, liquid or water-soluble powder, of the product. I treat the water four days a month — two days on, two days off and two days on again.

Terramycin and Neo-Terramycin are broad-spectrum antibiotic soluble powders without peer in stress prevention, growth promotion and diarrhea or scours prevention in my herd. Treatment of the water for one solid week a month has also boosted litter size, which is not surprising because it keeps the rabbits functioning in top condition. It also helps them convert feed better. It's a modern day medicine I wouldn't be without. I use a teaspoon of the soluble powder in every five gallons of water. I also water rabbits with Terramycin before and after a show, before I ship them and with the onset of a drastic change in the weather, all to alleviate stress. Again, get Terramycin from a rabbitry supply house for the best recommendations for use with rabbits.

Before the litter pops out of the box I use a Lysol solution, rinsed and rinsed and rinsed, on the wire hutch floor to minimize the chances of the litter picking up disease organisms that may be lurking there. Other disinfectants work well. Some raisers sear the floor with a propane torch. The idea is to kill the germs.

The Emtryl soluble powder is used to prevent the number one killer of rabbits, mucoid enteritis. Not everyone will admit it, but the fact is that there has been no known effective treatment of mucoid enteritis until very recently, when a British veterinarian tested Emtryl on a colony of 230 New Zealand White and crossbred rabbits. I have used it only for a short time but am convinced of its value.

First of all, let's take a look at mucoid enteritis. This is a form of diarrhea that hits young rabbits between five to eight weeks of age, primarily. It can kill them in 24 hours. Today, the young bunny looks great, bouncing around the hutch. Tonight, he's thin, scruffy-coated, wet around the mouth, squinty-eyed and sitting listlessly in a corner, perhaps with its feet in the water crock. It usually emits a steady stream of jelly-like feces that foul its complete rear underside. If you pick him up and shake him up and down you hear a splashing sound within. Tomorrow morning, he's dead.

And the next day another may go. And another, a couple of days later. You may lose an entire litter. And until recently, there hasn't been much you could do about it.

I will say that good clean draft-free quarters, a good diet, the regular use of sulfaquinoxaline sodium and Terramycin and a nest box that keeps the bunnies inside until as close to three weeks of age as possible are all helpful. I've even had some good luck with oral antibiotic baby pig dosers. Medicated rabbit pellets have also helped, I'm sure. But the fact remains — mucoid enteritis has confounded rabbit raisers.

Emtryl soluble powder is the Salsbury Laboratories brand name for the generic drug dimetridazole. It comes in a 6.42 ounce packet. I dissolve the packet in 17½ gallons of water (or a quarter of it in 4¾ gallons) and give continuously to the litters of 4-6 week-old rabbits as the sole source of water. This means I close off their automatic watering valve, and use a crock. None of these rabbits is used for meat for well over a month after withdrawal of the drug, but a word of caution and some digression is needed here. According to the vet who tested the product in England, this drug is eliminated from the tissues of the *pig* in seven days. In the United States this product is approved by the Food and Drug Administration only for *turkey* blackhead disease, and a withdrawal of five days before slaughter is required.

Neither in England nor the United States is this drug (nor many others) approved for use in *rabbits*.

In the United States, the Food and Drug Administration, and its Bureau of Veterinary Medicine, must approve all medications for animals, by species, before they may be sold. Few medications are approved for rabbits, because few drug companies are willing to stand the great expense of the testing required by species with little hope of return of their investment. They do not view the rabbit market as large enough to warrant the expenditure. So they don't test their products for rabbits and the government doesn't approve them for rabbits. But that doesn't mean they don't work on rabbits. They do, and they are sold by rabbitry supply houses. The big problem is that the rabbit industry has not sold itself as a market and therefore the drug companies don't know just what opportunities are available for selling the products.

Actually, only two groups know how to treat rabbits, and they won't or can't tell. Veterinarians won't; they want to do it themselves. The problem is that a rabbit can be replaced for the cost of a vet visit. Drug companies can't; the law won't allow it. Therefore, rabbit producers are left to wander from folklore that advocates vinegar and plasterboard, to rabbitry supply houses who have some good ideas and some good products but no real authority to sell them.

When I tell you that I use a certain product I say it works for me, and perhaps for others. My best recommendation is to take this up with a veterinarian. Let him prescribe treatment for you until you feel confident you can do it on your own. It will cost you something in the beginning, but it will pay off in the end.

Back to mucoid enteritis. If you can prevent it, and Emtryl has cut the incidence in more than half in tests, fine. There's no sense in trying to treat infected animals — not the young ones. Even if they live, which happens occasionally, they never amount to much. They are pinched and unthrifty; their growth is retarded. And you wouldn't want to breed such an animal — he might pass his susceptibility along.

Here are some other health problems you may encounter — and what to do about them:

Colds — a higher level of Terramycin. Use a teaspoon per gallon of water. Isolate the animal. If he doesn't respond in a couple of days, give an intramuscular injection of Combiotic.

Pneumonia — a Combiotic injection.

Sore hocks — treat as any abcess, using tincture of iodine or an antibiotic ointment. Give the rabbit a board to sit on.

Ear canker — drop some mineral oil or even salad or cooking oil into the ear daily until the mites that cause it are saturated and the crusty scales are gone. I've never had a rabbit with this problem and you shouldn't either, with wire floors.

There are of course a few other health problems. The only one I know that is contagious to man is ringworm. My best advice here is three-fold, and repetitious. Try to prevent disease and other health problems, not cure them. Consult your veterinarian. Get him to come out and see your rabbitry. Pay him his price. Deal with rabbitry supply houses for medications. You will find a list of these in the back of this book. The best for medications is New England Rabbitry Supply. Its catalog, which costs 50 cents, contains several pages of descriptions of diseases, symptoms, available products and directions for use. Get this catalog and study this section if no other. It's well worth the price.

SANITATION

Clean, dry hutches in a well-ventilated rabbitry will do more to maintain herd health than anything else. Keeping an all-wire hutch clean and dry is no problem. The urine and manure go right through the bottom. If they land in a well-drained pit below, inhabited by worms, two things will happen to help keep the rabbitry sanitary. The droppings will remain dry, in the first place, to hold odor down. And the worms will consume them, turning them to rich, black potting soil, further reducing odor and incidence of flies.

I don't recommend removal of manure from beneath the hutches daily or even once a week, particularly in warm weather. Moving it around causes unnecessary odor and it also prevents the worms from doing a good job. I remove manure only twice a year, in the fall and in the spring, on a cool, calm day. I do recommend application of a sprinkling of lime or superphosphate on the droppings once a week, especially in hot weather. This will hold odors down and improve the fertilizer value of the manure. Ordinarily, between the worms and the lime or superphosphate, the odor problem is non-existent. If smells should persist, however, there are a number of products available to help you. I prefer the dry granule forms that are sprinkled on the manure over the type that is mixed in water and poured or sprayed, because I believe in keeping the manure and the whole rabbitry as dry as possible. Dampness, of course, does not help eliminate odor. But dampness is not good for animal health, either. Purina Clean Air is a granulated odor control product that has served me well. I don't use much of it, but in periods of extra hot and humid weather it does a good job. Odor need not be a problem at all for you and certainly should not prevent anyone from keeping rabbits. Odor is not good for the rabbits and nobody else likes it either. It's up to the good rabbit raiser to eliminate it. The tools to do so are available, so there is no excuse for a bad-smelling rabbitry.

WHAT ABOUT FLIES?

Everyone knows flies breed in manure, among other places. But few flies appear in a rabbitry where the manure is dry and the worms are working. If they do cause a problem, spray the manure beds with a fly spray. Spray down on the manure so as not to contaminate the rabbits and their feed and water. It's a good idea to turn water crocks over and to spray before feeding pellets, when feeders are empty. This becomes less work if you have a piped, nipple-valve watering system because it is closed and protected from contamination.

Worms won't mind surface spraying because they are well beneath the top layer of manure. I spray manure beds three or four times a week during the hot summer months.

ANOTHER PEST

Mice can be a problem if you let them. If feed stands around in sacks, unprotected, mice will soon find it. I keep my feed in covered, galvanized garbage cans. Use of hopper feeders, which prevent spillage to the ground below, doesn't just save feed. It also keeps mice away. They will burrow under manure piles and come up looking for feed if it is spilled regularly. If you should be bothered by mice, put your pellets in metal cans for storage, and don't overfeed to the point that feed stands around waiting to be eaten by mice (or is scratched out). Then, get a good rat poison, such as D-Con, and spread it around the holes to their burrows under the manure. They won't be around much longer.

COMPLAINTS FROM NEIGHBORS, RELATIVES

A neat, attractive rabbitry — or one that can't even be seen — will minimize complaints from neighbors and a spouse or parent who has less enthusiasm for the creatures than you have. I like to keep a low profile in the neighborhood as far as rabbits are concerned. I don't realize any income from my neighbors, so there is no sense in talking up my rabbits with them. Also, I'm not interested in giving my rabbits away as pets to neighborhood youngsters, so I don't invite them all over to see the rabbitry. I do provide a couple of neighbors with compost for their flower beds and shrubbery, and vegetables that grow in my rabbit-composted garden, and if I raised more meat rabbits I'd offer them a fryer every now and then.

My rabbit shed in New Jersey sat among trees and shrubbery. I kept it painted green to blend with the surroundings. It looked like any tool shed in town. It could hardly be seen from my house in the summer when the trees wore their full foliage. A fence, flowers, or climbing vines would do the job as well, and I recommend such shading protection and camouflage, especially if you live in a residential area.

If you don't have a building, a good fence is a must to keep out marauding dogs, too. More grief has been caused in rabbitries by dogs than I care to recount. You simply must protect your rabbits from dogs. And this means building a fence.

Author's former backyard rabbitry in New Jersey.

Maintaining good relations with your neighbors is all-important. Rabbits that never caused an odor for years suddenly did so when the owner's son punched a neighbor's boy or tossed a rock through a window. If your neighbors don't like you, they may complain to the authorities about your rabbits. Many zoning laws are ambiguous and if the complaint is strong enough, it won't matter how neat and clean your rabbits are. You may be forced to get rid of them. So when you start with rabbits, don't make a big announcement in the neighborhood. Keep a neat, clean, odor-free rabbitry full of healthy and attractive rabbits, and stay in the good graces of your neighbors.

Rabbits may not be enjoyed as much by other members of your

family. But you can win them over in various ways. Income from my rabbitry goes toward future college expenses for my three children. But in the meantime, the rabbits endear themselves to the entire family by providing certain luxuries and treats we might not otherwise enjoy, or would have to fit into the family budget. As examples, our rabbits have bought the family restaurant dinners, big league baseball and Broadway play tickets, a grandfather clock, a 10-speed bicycle, a color television set, and, most recently, a Queen Anne lowboy. Members of my family have learned to appreciate rabbits.

10
On To
The Rabbit Shows!

Showing rabbits is only one reason for raising them, but for some raisers it is the only one. They love the fun and thrill of competing and winning. They enjoy spending a day with friends with the same interest. They often make show day a family outing with a tailgate picnic, a side fishing trip or local sightseeing.

One of the most rewarding aspects of rabbit shows is learning from the other breeders and the judges what you have done wrong and right so you can do it better before another show date arrives. And, of course, breeders who hope to sell breeding stock try to build a record of winning that will attract customers.

What can you win? There are trophies, ribbons, cash and special prizes put up by other competitors. There are breed club sweepstakes points and grand championship leg certificates and, simply, the judge's nod. Except for some state fair exhibitions, there is not a lot of money to be won, and this probably does more than anything else to keep rabbit shows as honest and fair as humans can make them. You will always find friendly competition — none of the brutally serious attitudes that prevail at dog or horse shows. You also will find extra nice, genuine, down-to-earth people among rabbit show-goers. I have been to horse shows around the country and to dog shows in Madison

Square Garden. At none of them have I found the fine class of competitors to be seen at rabbit shows. If you can't stand hypocrites and phonies, you probably hate dog and horse shows. But don't let that keep you away from the rabbit exhibitions. You will find a much better class of people.

LOCATING SHOWS

Rabbit shows do not receive a lot of publicity in the local newspapers. That's probably because they really are not spectator-oriented. They really are only fun for the competitors.

Local and state clubs and breed clubs sponsor the shows. If you belong to local and breed associations, you will learn about rabbit shows near you via club newsletters. If you belong to the ARBA, you will find a listing of upcoming shows in each issue of *Domestic Rabbits* magazine. These listings include the date of the show and the name and address of the show secretary.

HOW TO ENTER

Write the show secretary and ask to be put on the mailing list for the show catalog. There is no charge for this catalog, which gives directions to the show, the time to arrive, the entry fee and the prizes offered, and lists the breeds that are sanctioned, which means those breeds that will receive sweepstakes points. Any recognized standard breed may be shown, whether listed or not.

Fill out the enclosed entry blank and send it in as early as possible to ease the paperwork load of the secretary. Remember, he's a volunteer. Normally I don't enclose the entry fee in case some last-minute conflict should prevent me from attending. This fee, usually about $1.25 per rabbit, can be paid upon arrival at the show. Make a copy of the entry blank so that you won't have any mixups as to which rabbits you are entering.

On the day of the show, pack up your rabbits in crates or carriers that allow them enough room to turn around but not so much that they won't fit in the back or trunk of your car, where they will ride nicely if the day is not too warm. Most rabbit shows take place in the spring and the fall, but on a hot day keep your contestants as cool as possible. I use all-wire carriers that provide the same ventilation my hutches do. They are easy to make, or can be purchased.

SHOWROOM PROCEDURE

Most show secretaries specify in the catalog that you must arrive at least an hour before the judging starts. Upon arrival, get in line for your show cards and pay your entry fee.

At some shows, the rabbits are cooped and ear-marked by club members assigned the task. At the best-run local show I've ever attended, Tony Pisanelli's Green Mountain Rabbit Breeders spring show each Memorial Day weekend, your rabbits are even unloaded, fed and watered. But at most shows, rabbits remain in carrying cages and it's up to you to bring along a felt-tipped pen to mark their right ears with judging numbers and to fasten show cards to your carriers.

Be alert to announcements by the show superintendent. He will call for the various breeds to be brought to the show tables and it will be your responsibility, in many instances, to carry your own stock to the table.

The 1973 ARBA convention in Detroit

SHOWROOM CLASSES

Judges evaluate rabbits in classes, grouping them by breed, variety, age and sex. If you raise New Zealand Whites, for example, the first class on the table will be senior bucks — then senior does, six-to-eight-month bucks, 6-8 does, junior bucks and junior does and — perhaps —

Judging a Tan champion at the ARBA convention

pre-junior bucks and does. Seniors are eight months and over; 6-8s are 6-8s, juniors are under six months, and pre-juniors, if any, usually are about three months of age. Showroom classes for smaller breeds, such as Tans, are simpler. Seniors are over six months; juniors are under. In some shows, does and litters, and meat pens of three fryers each vie for prizes. Fur classes are also special, with separate entry fees, usually fifty cents. The prize money is a percentage of the entry fee. In fur classes, normal white fur, normal colored, Satin and Rex furs are judged separately. I like to enter Tans, which go in normal colored fur classes, because invariably they win. Tan fur, although classified as normal, exhibits greater sheen than that of any other rabbit, including the Satin. It's not unusual for Tans to cop all the top places in normal colored fur. I expect them to be put in a separate class of their own, like Satins and Rex, one of these days. In the meantime, at the expense of the other breeds, my Tans are cashing in.

CHOOSING THE WINNERS

A class of rabbits might contain, for example, 12 senior bucks. The judge looks them all over carefully and measures each individual's worth by two yardsticks. One is the *Standard* for the breed, which he

Author's son, John Bennett, admires trophies at a local rabbit show.

should know by heart. The other is *comparison* — one animal against another. One by one the rabbits are placed, from 12th to first, and the judge dictates remarks about each one's good and bad points to a recording secretary, who writes them on a show card that becomes the property of the animal's owner. The show secretary indicates placings on a show record sheet, from which he awards trophies, ribbons and special prizes and makes his report to the exhibitors and to the breed clubs. If the show secretary does not issue you a complete report of the show (and most report only what *you* have won), you can find a comprehensive account in the newsletter of the breed specialty club. To receive this newsletter, of course, you must be a club member.

ON TO VICTORY

Let's say your senior buck wins its class of twelve. If there were at least two other exhibitors, you have won a "leg" on a grand championship. Two more legs wins you a grand championship certificate. But that means winning at two more shows. It's not easy.

Your first senior buck is held aside by the judge until he chooses the first senior doe, 6-8 buck and doe and junior winners. He then looks them all over on the table together and chooses the best New Zealand

White. If it's your buck, he becomes Best of Variety, probably wins a rosette ribbon and is held aside until the class and variety winners of New Zealand Red and Black varieties are chosen. He then selects the best New Zealand. If your white buck wins, you'll probably get a trophy. If they are picking a Best in Show winner, he can compete against the best of the other breeds, perhaps for a silver cup or a similarly sought-after prize. If you take *that* home, you doubtless will consider your time and effort at raising rabbits well spent indeed!

Actually, there are other prizes to be won. If, for example, your buck had lost out to a doe for Best of Variety or Best of Breed, then it might have won the consolation Best of Opposite Sex, which usually gets a trophy also. As I write this, I'm counting four trophies won this spring, as I have attended four shows and won Best of Breed at two, and Best of Opposite Sex at the other two. I'll attend one more show this spring, that Green Mountain show in Vermont, and I hope to maintain my winning pace at the expense of the fine New England breeders.

If I do, I'll be pleased, but not too jubilant. And if I don't, I'll be disappointed, but not distraught. I've learned not to be too happy if I win, nor too sad if I lose. The judges are all too human. If I win, the judge is one of the best. If I lose, he has a lot to learn. Seriously, the judge's verdict is not the last word. If you win consistently, over a period of time, under a number of judges, you can begin to take real pride in your herd. But isolated, individual verdicts should never influence your opinion of your stock. Never breed rabbits according to a judge's verdict. You are your own best judge when it comes to selecting breeders. (P.S. You guessed it. One of my Tans won Best of Breed in Vermont on Memorial Day.)

SELECTING SHOW STOCK

You are the only judge when it comes to choosing which of your rabbits to enter in shows. As you breed, you will want to keep an eye on the calendar for spring and fall show dates. Try to breed for animals that will be at the top of the age limit for their classes, e.g., 5½-month juniors, 7½-month 6-8s. Don't show seniors over a year or two, however, as they probably won't do as well as they did in their youth. Practically never will you win with a doe that has brought up a family.

Fur and flesh condition are two prime considerations. Don't enter a rabbit if it isn't in the peak of condition because the judge will give it short shrift. Also, watch for disqualifying features, such as bad teeth, spots of the wrong color fur, off-color eyes or toenails. You must be familiar with the Standard for your breed. The complete *Standard of Perfection* is available from the ARBA.

HOW MANY TO ENTER?

You may enter as many rabbits as you like, in an effort to improve your chances of winning. I know one man who enters hundreds at a single show. Most breeders enter from two or three to about 20 or so.

You may want to enter only the very best you have, thereby holding your entries to a minimum. After all, only one rabbit is Best of Breed. Or, you might want the judge's opinion of a great number of your rabbits, or desire to amass sweepstakes points to win a breed club trophy. It also depends upon how many good ones you have and how many you can transport. This spring I have entered as few as two in a distant show, and as many as 25 in one close to home.

Neil Townsend with his Best of Breed Lilac Rabbit at the 1973 ARBA convention.

Sue Atwell shows her Best of Breed French Lop at the Detroit convention in 1973.

WATCH THEM IN THE NEST BOX

Watch your young show prospects from an early age — even in the nest box. At weaning time, hold the best prospects for shows and keep several for some weeks before narrowing your choice of show candidates. Actually, you only breed from those you feel will produce good show stock, but you will have to choose the best among the offspring.

CONDITIONING FOR THE SHOW TABLE

Once you have selected your candidates, give them special attention for weeks and even months before the show. Put them in the best possible fur and flesh condition. Successful exhibitors all have their own formulas for feeding for top condition, and I'm no different. Here are some of the steps I take toward the trophies.

— Mixed, coarse horse feed with molasses is a great fur conditioner. So is wheat germ oil on top of rabbit pellets. Also sunflower seeds.

— Milk and mangels plus oats will put weight on those that need it. Dry, powdered milk is not expensive. A lot depends on how badly you want to win. If milk pays off with a big win and breeding stock sales, it's cheap, indeed.

— Brushing with a curved wire tine slicker brush, followed by a bristle brush, will speed a rabbit through a change of coat.

— *Regular* feeding and a constant source of water does more, of course, to keep rabbits in top condition, than anything else I know.

WHAT IT'S ALL ABOUT

There's no denying the ultimate satisfaction of winning an annual ARBA convention or the season's first local show — and proving to yourself that you have outdone your fellow breeders from the nest box to the show table. It's the same thrill that goes to a Kentucky Derby-winning stable owner or the builder of the car that captures the Indianapolis 500. For a lot of breeders, it's what it's all about. But every breeder, whether he shows or not, should keep his stock in winning condition. And every breeder should give the shows a whirl.

11
Rabbit Associations

Hundreds of rabbit associations exist in the United States and they benefit their members in several important ways at the local, state, regional and national levels. In addition, they offer their members the opportunity to advance the cause of rabbits in general and favorite breeds in particular.

The American Rabbit Breeders Association Inc., which maintains a full-time, paid secretary and office staff in Bloomington, Illinois, is the parent organization. Affiliated with ARBA on the national level are breed specialty clubs dedicated to the advancement of the individual breeds. Geographically, there are regional, state and local associations also affiliated with the ARBA.

The ARBA holds an annual meeting and convention show each year, usually in October or November. Members enter many thousands of rabbits in this week-long show, the biggest of all United States rabbit competitions.

The breed specialty clubs also conduct meetings at these annual conventions, and usually hold a show devoted exclusively to their breed at some other time of the year as well. The rest of the year the ARBA and the breed specialty clubs maintain communications with their members through the *Domestic Rabbits* magazine and the specialty club newsletters. I'm especially familiar with this procedure, having founded *Domestic Rabbits* and served as its first editor, and because recently I edited and mailed the newsletter read by members of the American Tan Rabbit Club.

REGIONAL GROUPS

At the regional, state and local levels, club meetings are more frequent, usually once a month for local clubs. Members assemble at a centrally located meeting room and discuss various aspects of rabbit raising. Rabbits are bought and sold, and marketing, breeding, management and every other imaginable tidbit of information is exchanged. Each local, state or regional association conducts one or two shows·per year, which requires much planning and work by volunteers from the ranks. In addition, newsletters keep members informed about club activities, including an annual social event, such as a picnic or a dinner, as well as tips on rabbit raising in general.

Every successful rabbit raiser I know maintains close contact with other breeders in the various associations because of the invaluable exchange of information that takes place. What is difficult to make clear to some breeders is that membership fees license them to help the association; the fees don't entitle them to any great largess. These are amateur, volunteer associations of individual breeders working together for the common good at each level, with the exception of ARBA staff, part-time payment to some secretaries and the handful of commercial rabbit cooperatives scattered across the country, some of which have paid workers in their processing plants.

ARBA BENEFITS

ARBA members are entitled to register rabbits, earn grand championship certificates, vote for officers and directors and generally have a voice in the direction the rabbit fancy is taking. Membership at present is a very low $7 per year, which includes a copy of the 200-page book *Official Guide to Raising Better Rabbits,* and a subscription to *Domestic Rabbits* magazine. Members also receive the *Yearbook,* which is a directory of all the members in the United States and abroad, and also contains the Constitution and Bylaws of the Association. If a breeder is not a member of the ARBA, he is not up to date on what's happening in the world of rabbits. In fact, at this writing, membership will bring with it the only nationally circulated, regularly published magazine devoted exclusively to rabbits. I couldn't afford not to belong and neither could the other 20,000 members.

12
The Future Of
The Rabbit Industry

In the previous chapter, you have seen that several hundred rabbit breeders associations exist in this country. But there is still a need for another, or so it would seem. Except for a few local commercial cooperatives, there is no group dedicated to the promotion of the rabbit for the purpose to which it is best suited — to be eaten.

Within the American Rabbit Breeders Association there are a number of committees and departments, including a commercial department. But mere volunteers in the commercial department haven't the ability or the equipment to promote rabbit meat and, unfortunately, neither do the leaders of the ARBA. Therefore the ARBA and affiliated organizations devote 99 per cent of their effort to promotion of the fancy side, the showing, of rabbits. That is not all bad, because it is from the fanciers that commercial rabbit breeders obtain their foundation stock, and a good, solid fancy element is needed. And it is there, having been well provided by the ARBA and affiliated organizations for a great many years.

It strikes me, however, that the best *single goal* of the ARBA would be to increase the demand for rabbit meat by the American housewife. The way to do this would be to start still another organization, one which might be called the American Commercial Rabbit Council. Inasmuch as there is practically no demand for rabbit meat in this country in comparison with other meats (per capita annual consumption of beef in the U.S. is 117 pounds; of rabbit, 2 *ounces!*), this demand would have to be created. Critics of the idea say there is no sense in creating the demand, because as prolific as rabbits are, there is not a large enough supply. Of course, there is only one answer to such a chicken and egg question. There is only one thing that creates a *supply* of anything. That is, quite simply, *demand.*

What would happen if rabbit meat found its way to the American dinner table on a regular basis?

1. More rabbits would be raised.
2. More breeding stock would be needed.
3. More rabbit feed would be produced and volume production would affect the price favorably.
4. More wire hutches, feeders, watering equipment, nest boxes and sundry other equipment would be manufactured and sold and the price would be affected favorably by volume manufacture and sales.
5. More animal health companies would research, clear with the Food and Drug Administration, and market health and nutrition products for rabbits. Thus, the task of keeping rabbits healthy and productive would be easier; medicine for rabbits would become widely available where it currently is practically nonexistent, and veterinarians would have more interest, information and expertise.
6. Government, university and industry research into rabbit breeding and management would increase. Thus, rabbit raising would become a more exact animal science and be more pleasurable and profitable for all engaged in it.

The ultimate beneficiary would be the consumer, who would find delicious, nutritious rabbit abundantly available to provide a welcome mealtime change of pace at a competitive price.

It seems to me that any person who believes rabbits are mainly for eating (as I do) would agree that the foregoing half-dozen points are desirable and reasonable. Even those who are strictly fanciers (of which I am one) would have to agree, I think, that at least some are desirable. For example, with more breeding stock needed, fanciers would find a greater market awaiting their production, enjoy lower feed prices, more and better equipment and advances in health and management practices. Part-time breeders who always wanted to expand into full-time operation would have a sufficient market to warrant the move. Others would be able to breed more often, being better assured of a demand.

Demand is the key word. Could such a demand be created? I am sure of it. Publicity and promotion could do the job. Florida oranges, California prunes and catfish are examples of agricultural products that recently have benefited from promotion. Beef, our favorite meat, receives a couple of million dollars worth of promotion every year, but rabbit, known but to few, gets next to nothing. The Pel-Freez Company, which sells frozen rabbit meat nationally, takes small ads in some women's magazines from time to time. Except for a few hundred dollars in bumper stickers and similar materials for National Rabbit Week, which occurs during the summer when most of America is on vacation, the ARBA spends nothing.

An organized and professionally executed publicity and promotion plan would achieve the six goals I've mentioned (and more). And it would be good for rabbit raisers as well as consumers. But there's yet another group that should be interested, because it would be absolutely terrific for them. Who are they?

They are the nation's largest milling companies — Ralston Purina, Carnation Albers, Allied Mills, to name a few. They are also the industry's largest equipment suppliers — Valentine Equipment Company, Bass Equipment Company, Favorite Manufacturing, Glick Manufacturing Company, Circle K. etc. They are also the laboratories, processors and commercial breeders.

Companies in the above categories would gain the most if rabbit meat consumption increased, because they would make more money. They would sell more feed and equipment. Processors would sell more meat. Commercial growers would sell more rabbits.

It stands to reason that the people who have the most to gain from an expanded demand for rabbit meat have the best reason for making it happen. Here's where the ARBA could come in. ARBA could unite those who supply the breeders, in a special unit of ARBA that might be called the American Commercial Rabbit Council (or something of that sort). The Council would hire a public relations agency to promote rabbit meat at a rate that would keep demand just ahead of supply.

Such a campaign would begin regionally, in regional media, at a moderate pace, and eventually expand across the nation in national media, increasing demand at a rate that would give breeders and processors time to tool up to meet it. (In the case of rabbits, that wouldn't take too much time because of the animal's renowned reputation for fast maturity and reproduction.) A public relations firm could handle the job.

So it would be the task of those who would form such an ARBA American Commercial Rabbit Council to gather members, who would be required to hold ARBA membership, solicit the funds and spend the money wisely to increase the demand for rabbit meat.

Who would do the work to form such a council? In the past several years I have discussed this idea with three agencies who have expressed a great deal of interest. One has submitted to me a detailed plan. Another is already successfully operating such a council in another branch of the food supply sector. All three are successful firms ready and willing to go to work.

This work can't be done successfully by part-time volunteers such as those who man the various fancier organizations. It requires full-time professionals with a profit motive. They will take on the job if it looks as though they can make money at it. And to the three I have contacted, it looks good.

All this would take a little seed money, about $5,000, but it can be seen that if money ever made more money, it could be here. Therefore, the Council members would support the cause in direct proportion to the benefit they derive from the industry. As an example, a small raiser, who produces no more than 300 rabbits per year, pays dues of $7 per year to belong to ARBA. He gets more than his money's worth. But suppose he was the nation's largest supplier of rabbit feed. What would his ARBA dues be? Right, still $7. But what should they be if ARBA was actually helping him sell this feed by expanding the demand for rabbit meat? Certainly more than $7. Perhaps several hundred or a thousand dollars or more per year.

One corporation that belongs to ARBA at $7 per year also belongs to several other livestock organizations. To one of these it pays dues of $24,000 per year! Of course, it gets its money's worth, or it wouldn't pay the price. But the point is, if it does get its money's worth, it will pay.

Before the United States rabbit industry can ever become viable, before rabbit meat becomes part of the American family diet, the ARBA will have to start the ball rolling, will have to provide some seed money for a meat promotion effort. So far it has shown little interest, officially, although many of the members are in favor of such a plan.

In 1974 I proposed this idea to the members of the ARBA through articles in *Domestic Rabbits* magazine. More than 100 members responded with letters and many others spoke to me about it at rabbit shows. All but four favored the idea. Three of them were processors, and of course, it was a plan for breeders, not processors, and the idea of promoting meat nationally would appeal less to a processor who is already selling locally and only would have to withstand competition under such a plan.

Here's what a few of the ARBA members told me:

"I'm behind you 100 per cent. Thank you for some great articles." — Florida.

"Ribbons don't pay the grain. I say yes spend the $5,000 and help us sell meat." — Massachusetts.

"Man, am I glad someone has finally found the front end of the problem in the rabbit industry. Your idea is just great." — Florida.

"My feed company here said it would get behind something like this, too. Many would profit, not just rabbit raisers." — Minnesota.

"I do not have a lot of New Zealands but would expand if I could be sure of a market for them." — Iowa.

"Go gettum boy. We've been messin' around too long." — Oregon.

"The soundest proposal I've heard of. Every rabbit breeder stands to gain. We need this. There is no way to lose." — Montana.

"I don't believe ARBA could use its funds for a better purpose." — Kansas.

"If we don't promote rabbits in a good professional way we will never get to first base with them." — Minnesota.

"I sure hope this will be the year to promote the rabbit." — Louisiana.

"I joined the ARBA in the hope that it would promote the commercial aspect of this business and I think we're finally seeing the light." — Michigan.

"To me this is one of the very best ideas that has yet come forth for the rabbit industry." — Kentucky.

"I am all for getting a *market* for rabbits. I have 50 I want to get rid of now. No sale!" — Michigan.

"Other livestock organizations really promote. Why not the ARBA? Take the money and go." — New York.

"I believe promote the food as much as the fancy — The rabbit more than the association." — Georgia.

"This idea will help the commercial grower better than any other idea." — Missouri.

"Full steam ahead. We're forty years behind now." — Illinois.

"I live in an area that has a lot of publicity for pork and beef and I can readily see the sound sense in this project." — Nebraska.

"I sell to Pel-Freez. I think your idea is a good one and I support you 100 per cent." — Oklahoma.

"Public Relations is the answer. I stand behind you." — Tennessee.

"This would be good for all the breeders in the country." — Oklahoma.

"Let's start a massive campaign to get Americans to start eating rabbit meat." — Connecticut.

"You gave me the idea to go to our local feed stores and ask them to join our local club. I think you should go ahead and spend the money." — Ohio

And so the letters went. But while the membership of ARBA seems overwhelmingly in favor of this idea, the leadership is not, preferring to remain a strictly fancier organization. Yet the rabbit holds great possibilities as a meat animal for Americans. And so it seems obvious that in time the ARBA will either have to organize a commercial unit or find that someone else will come along and do it.

There exists, therefore, a fine opportunity for someone to enlist the aid of a trade association management team to solicit funds from companies already used to paying them to promote livestock sales, and to put a new meat product on the table in America. The fact is that it will never happen until a trade association is formed by ARBA or another group. There exists no nationally successful industry without national promotion.

Perhaps the main reason that a single goal of rabbit meat promotion has not yet been sought is simply because the rabbit has so many diverse uses. It is so versatile — just like the Shmoo to which I alluded at the beginning of this book. And thus it is difficult to get agreement to work toward a single goal. Those of us who have rabbits see them in so many different ways that we can't yet see eye to eye on promoting them. But one of these days, I believe, we will all agree that those in a position to get the most out of the rabbit industry are the ones who should put the most into it.

13
Cooking Rabbit
The Modern Way

One taste will convince you that more domestic rabbit should be eaten. A whole lot of people are missing out on a good thing. It's not easy, however, to get some people to take that first bite.

For example, my children would *never* eat rabbit. Perish the thought. They do eat a lot of chicken, though, and occasionally inquire where, perchance, the wings might be, and how come there are extra drumsticks.

My reply, of course, is that should a person care to purchase certain chicken parts he can do so, snubbing wings, backs, necks, etc. Thus reassured, they take another bite of rabbit.

Domestic rabbit meat is fine-grained and pearly white. It does not taste wild or gamey, as some believe. The reason is, quite simply, that the domestic rabbit is no more wild game than a Black Angus steer or a Rhode Island Red rooster.

Before you start raising rabbits for meat, you certainly should taste it. So I suggest you purchase a Pel-Freez fryer-broiler, available at chain supermarkets across America, found in the frozen food case. The price might surprise you. Usually it has been the same price as top round steak. The price has a lot to do with the feed/meat conversion ratio, which we discussed earlier, plus the costs of processing, packaging, shipping, etc., not forgetting a profit for the grower and the processor and the retailer. This cost would be about 50 cents per pound if you raise your own.

CHICKEN IS CHEAPER

A lot of people compare rabbit to chicken, and of course the price per pound of chicken is much lower — two-thirds to three-quarters lower. This is due partly to the absolutely amazing performance of the American poultry industry. Chicken actually costs less today than it did 25 years ago. How many items on your grocery list — or any other shopping list — can make that claim? I know of none, although in spite of the gripes of the uninformed, food remains quite a bargain in this country, taking a smaller percentage of our income than it does in any other country in the world, and even a smaller portion of our paycheck than it did years ago.

Commercially packaged rabbit as can be found in the grocer's freezer.

RABBIT LAGS BEHIND

The tortoise-paced rabbit industry will have to make some giant hops to catch chicken's feed conversion ratio of about 2:1 (compared to 4:1 for rabbit), largely brought about over the years by superb geneticists who so far have not yet turned their talents over to the rabbit.

But rabbit has finer bones than chicken and the meat has a finer grain, shorter fiber and a chewier texture, so a little fills you up a lot.

The U.S. Navy recognized this some years ago when it served rabbit and allotted each sailor a six-ounce portion, compared to twelve ounces when serving chicken.

HIGH-PROTEIN, LOW-CALORIE RABBIT

In addition, domestic rabbit is extremely low in calories and high in protein content.

Here is a U.S. Department of Agriculture statistical breakdown of several meats:

	Protein	Fat	Moisture	Calories Per Pound
Rabbit	20.8	10.2	27.9	795
Chicken	20.0	11.0	67.6	810
Veal (medium fat)	18.8	14.0	66.0	910
Turkey (medium fat)	20.1	22.2	58.3	1190
Beef	16.3	28.0	55.0	1440
Lamb (medium fat)	15.7	27.7	55.8	1420
Pork (medium fat)	11.9	45.0	42.0	2050

You can see from this table that rabbit has *more protein* and *fewer calories* than *any* of the popular meats! It also contains less moisture, which means you don't purchase water. Neither do you pay for the skin, which, in the case of chicken, many find fatty and rubbery, and pay for it only to throw it away.

IT'S SO DIGESTIBLE

Rabbit is easy to digest. Remember this when feeding children, senior citizens or those with weak stomachs. Those on bland, soft-food ulcer diets take well to the tender texture, mild flavor and easy digestibility of domestic rabbit.

PREPARING FOR COOKING

When I butcher a fryer-broiler, I cut up the pieces, rinse them thoroughly in cold water, and chill a couple of hours in the refrigerator. I don't soak them in water. Usually my wife, Alice, takes over here and prepares it for the freezer. Ordinarily, all my meat rabbits get a stay in the freezer. Alice says it stays there until we forget which one it is. We never eat a rabbit we know personally.

Uncooked rabbit, washed and chilled, may be frozen whole or in parts. Use moisture-vapor-resistant material suitable for freezing. Alice uses plastic freezer bags, but you can use heavy-duty aluminum foil or freezer paper. Be sure to squeeze the air out of the package before sealing.

Prepare cooked rabbit for freezing the same way except when you include gravy or sauce. Alice suggests packing it in rigid containers with tight lids, although I've never seen her freeze cooked rabbit. Somebody eats it up first.

Fresh rabbit will store in the freezer for four to six months; cooked rabbit, about two months.

THAWING RABBIT

It's best to thaw rabbit in the refrigerator, with the wrapping loosened. Pieces will thaw in four to nine hours; whole rabbits may take 12 to 16 hours — the bigger, the longer. To thaw faster, plop the rabbit, bag and all, in cold water. Don't re-freeze either cooked or uncooked rabbit once it has been thawed. Successive thawing and re-freezing lowers quality.

When it comes to storage, keep in mind that an entire rabbit or two makes a meal for the whole family. If you butcher a hog or a steer you have a storage problem. But rabbits store very nicely on the hoof in the hutch. You can pick one out, cook it up and it's gone at one sitting.

In spite of all the disparaging comments about chicken, it's well to remember that you can cook rabbit according to almost any chicken recipe. And, you can also prepare some veal-type dishes with rabbit. You can cook it fancy or plain, and the following are just a few samples of the hundreds of recipes you can use. Many can be had for free by writing to either Pel-Freez or the ARBA. Addresses are in the back of this book.

ALICE BENNETT'S CRISPY "OVEN-FRIED" RABBIT
(The Children's Favorite)

2 cups finely crushed potato chips
1 egg, well beaten
¼ cup butter or oleomargarine
1 fryer-broiler rabbit (2-2½ pounds dressed) cut in serving pieces

Dip rabbit pieces in beaten egg, then coat with potato chips. Melt butter or oleo in shallow baking pan. Arrange rabbit pieces in pan and bake in 375-degree oven 30 minutes. Turn rabbit and bake another 30 minutes or until well done. What you've got is "fried" rabbit without all the grease.

GOLDEN BROWN FRIED RABBIT

1 rabbit fryer, cut up
½ cup flour
1½ teaspoons salt
½ tsp. pepper
butter or fat

Moisten rabbit meat, drain, but do not dry. Shake pieces in paper bag in mixture of flour and seasoning. Place pieces in ½ inch hot butter or fat in heavy skillet, turning to brown evenly on all sides. Reduce heat, cover and cook slowly 40 to 50 minutes or until tender. For crisp crust on rabbit meat, uncover for the last 10 to 15 minutes.

BRAISED RABBIT

½ cup flour
1½ tsp. thyme leaves, crumbled
1 tsp. salt
½ tsp. onion salt
½ tsp. celery salt
1/8 tsp. pepper
2 rabbit fryers (about 2 pounds each) cut up
¼ cup shortening
1 cup water

Put flour and spices in a plastic bag. Add rabbit pieces and toss to coat well with flour mixture. Heat shortening in skillet. Add rabbit, turning to brown on all sides. Add water, cover and simmer until rabbit is tender. You may also thicken the cooking liquid for a delightful gravy. Alice likes to serve this in the summer with vegetables from our garden. Son Bob contributes the thyme from his herb garden near the back door. He says that's why it tastes so good.

RABBIT CASSEROLE

2 rabbit fryers (about 2 pounds each), cut up
4 slices bacon
3 medium size onions, quartered
2 green peppers, cut up
1 clove garlic, crushed
½ cup white wine
1 can (1 pound) whole tomatoes
1 can condensed cream of mushroom soup
1 tsp. salt
1 tsp. marjoram, crushed
1 tsp. thyme, crushed

Sauté bacon until crisp. Drain on paper towels and set aside. Brown rabbit a few pieces at a time in bacon drippings, then arrange in a 10-cup baking or casserole dish. Add onion, green pepper and garlic to same skillet and add wine. Cook, stirring and crushing tomatoes until slightly thickened (about 5 minutes). Then stir in cream of mushroom soup, marjoram and thyme. Heat to boiling, stirring frequently. Spoon over rabbit in baking dish and cover.

Bake at 350 degrees one hour until rabbit is tender. Just before serving, crumble reserved bacon and sprinkle over the rabbit and vegetables. Serve with hot buttered rice or noodles.

ITALIAN RABBIT WITH SPAGHETTI [Rabbit Cacciatore]

1 rabbit fryer cut in serving pieces
1 large onion
2 8-ounce cans tomato paste
½ tsp. garlic salt
½ tsp. oregano
2 bay leaves
½ tsp. sugar
salt and pepper to taste
spaghetti, 8 or 9 ounce package, boiled

Put rabbit in salted boiling water and simmer until tender. When cooked, remove meat from bones if desired. Combine all other ingredients, except spaghetti with rabbit broth and simmer for one hour. Return rabbit to sauce. Serve on a bed of spaghetti.

You can find a recipe for hasenpfeffer in almost any cookbook. Also, you can barbecue rabbit in the back yard just like chicken. I like to parboil it, cook it inside some aluminum foil with the sauce, and then brown it up while basting with more sauce, right over the coals. I'm sure all the good cooks get the idea that rabbit can be prepared in a great many delicious ways, fancy or just down home.

Afterword

What kind of people raise rabbits? Are any of them like you? And why do they raise rabbits? Answers to these questions may help you envision yourself as a successful rabbit raiser.

Take the New Jersey friend of mine who is a family man in his thirties, with a position in the purchasing department of a local firm. He started only a couple of years ago to raise a few rabbits for his own table in a neat little storage shed behind the split-level home in his suburban back yard. His goal is to put a rabbit on the table each week. Not only has he reached his objective, thereby making a dent in his meat bill, he also sells breeding stock and extra fryers to a butcher. In addition, he is a frequent winner of blue ribbons at regional rabbit shows. His success arrived soon because of his ability to see the necessity of starting right. He purchased foundation stock from the nation's top producer of his chosen breed. Then he housed, fed and managed these rabbits in the most modern way.

I have another friend in Vermont, about the same age. He is a professional in a utility company, the father of two school-age youngsters and a resident of one of the larger towns. He has raised rabbits for several years. He has always insisted upon the very best rabbits available and kept his rabbitry, which is in one half of a detached two-car garage, scrupulously clean. People actually wait for his rabbits to be born to purchase them for their own rabbitries. But his standards are so high that only the very best of his production is sold for breeding stock. The rest go for meat. He butchers some for his own table because his family really enjoys rabbit.

But they also like a good steak once in a while, just like anybody else. So, in a satisfying arrangement for all concerned, the Vermonter swaps dressed rabbit meat, pound for pound, to the operator of a freezer locker, for beef. His friends and neighbors know he raises rabbits in his garage. But I call him a cattle raiser.

A professor of animal husbandry at the University of Maine pioneered the importation of my favorite fancy breed into the United States from England and Holland. He has steadily improved this breed by careful mating and study over many years. Last year the association that sponsors the breed in this country voted him their most outstanding member and presented him with a handsome plaque to prove it.

A Long Island airline pilot and his family are also avid fanciers. Both a dentist and a waitress in New Jersey lead 4-H clubs dedicated to raising rabbits and they teach many youngsters what they need to know to be successful at the 4-H shows each year. The waitress has written two fine manuals for the young people in her club. The dentist shows his charges how to build the most advanced rabbit housing available.

A pharmacist produces laboratory stock in Puerto Rico; so does a factory worker in Maryland, a carpenter in Pennsylvania and a farmer in New Hampshire. A New York City marketing executive raises breeding stock, show stock and meat rabbits at his home in suburbia. And he still has plenty of time to play golf. An Oregon family — he's a sculptor and a government administrator; she's a weaver and the head of her own mail order business; their daughter is a high school student — raise many fancy breeds successfully and fill orders for breeding stock from all over the country (and Canada). They will beat you at shows. At one show last year they took home the top trophy in each of 10 different breeds!

A nearby teacher, his wife and twin sons spend a lot of time together at the shows, where their stock is always among the best to be seen. A metals company executive is also a back yard raiser.

A monk keeps his rabbits behind the garden in the monastery. Unfortunately, his rabbits are so handsome they sell at a nice profit. Unfortunately, because his profits have compromised his vow of poverty. A minister is losing money on rabbits but doesn't mind a bit. He heads a home for orphaned boys. He bought them rabbits and hutches to teach them animal husbandry and business principles. So far, they are still in the red. But the minister is all smiles. Those boys are really busy and he loves it.

A surgeon, a chiropractor, a lawyer and an ex-convict, and a man who has sewn the bristles into brushes for 30 years are all successful rabbit raisers. Two Boy Scouts recently spent several months raising rabbits to earn a merit badge. I served as their counselor, after devising the requirements and writing a book on rabbit raising for the Boy

Scouts of America. Pursuit of the same merit badge (via earlier and *easier* requirements) in 1948 started me raising rabbits myself.

A few years ago, an attractive young woman in New York State learned how to hand spin wool. Now she raises Angora rabbits and spins their wool into yarn. Her ability is so envied that she teaches hand spinning, dyeing and weaving in her own studio and at two colleges, two art centers and a museum.

I could cite cases of many more people who have made a success of rabbit raising on a small scale, but you may be wondering if it is possible to really make it big with rabbits. Sure, it's possible, and the chances are improving each year, but it takes a special person to make it big at most anything. The production of livestock is one of the most challenging such areas.

One of the most special people ever to raise rabbits was Edward H. Stahl, who died in 1973 at the age of 87. I had the privilege of knowing Mr. Stahl, who preceded me as a publicity worker on behalf of the ARBA and who gave me a lot of guidance. I consider Ed Stahl to be the single most important man in the development of the United States rabbit industry.

Ed Stahl was born in New York State in 1886. At the age of 20 he left home and hired on as a deckhand with a tramp steamer. It was scheduled to go to New Orleans, but he left the ship early and rode a freight train to Kansas City, Mo. In nearby Holmes Park he got a job in a foundry, married, and bought two acres behind the foundry. A co-worker offered Ed a pair of rabbits. He housed them in a rundown corncrib in 1913 and by 1928 he had spent so much time with them that his boss told him he had to make a choice between the job and the rabbits.

"I chose rabbits," Ed said, having built a rabbit business that was grossing $350,000 per year. At one time he had 65 full-time employees and a second rabbitry in New York State. He sold breeding stock through the Sears & Roebuck catalog and in a single month sold $49,000 worth. It is said that Ed Stahl, with his rabbit sales and associated activities, which included publishing and the manufacture of supplies, became a millionaire. Is that what you mean by really making it big with rabbits?

Many Americans have achieved success with rabbits, because the rabbit has so much going for it. But it is perhaps because it looks so easy to raise rabbits right that many of those who try fail in discouragement in a very short time. One vital aspect lies hidden beneath that soft and furry exterior — the necessity for starting right and raising them the modern way.

Reading
About Rabbits

The following list of books, booklets, pamphlets, magazines and newspapers includes only those that I have read myself and found useful.

BOOKS

Bob Bennett's Guide to Winning Rabbit Shows. My latest rabbit book, all about getting into showing rabbits. Published by Dorn Publishing Co. 66 Pages, $2.95 plus 50¢ postage from Bob Bennett, One Governor's Lane, Shelburne VT 05482.

The next nine books are available from New England Rabbitry Supply, Dept. B, RFD 3, North Middleboro, Mass. 02346.

Domestic Rabbit Production, George Templeton. 209 pages, hard cover. Very complete book, based on years of experience as director of U.S. Rabbit Experiment Station (closed several years ago). Methods and equipment somewhat dated. First written in 1955. Latest revision 1968.

The Private Life of the Rabbit, R.M. Lockley. 200 pages, hard cover. A new book by an English naturalist, and only about wild rabbits, but nevertheless provides insights not found elsewhere.

How to Start a Commercial Rabbitry, Paul Mannell. 100 pages, soft cover. Apparently written to sell equipment, which is advertised therein, but still a handy little book for anyone who wants to produce meat.

Practical Inbreeding, W. Watmough. 67 pages, printed in England. What inbreeding does for all livestock; successful inbreeding. One of the best books for a beginner.

The Book of the Tan Rabbit, A.S. Howden. 50 pages, printed in England. Author bred some of the ancestors of my Tans. He provides specific information on Tans but also good general breeding and management tips.

The Book of the Dutch Rabbit, James Read. 32 pages, printed in England. Does for Dutch what Howden book does for Tans.

Modern Angora Wool Farming, Carl Nagel. 90 pages. Poorly printed, but a useful little volume for those interested in Angoras.

Green Foods for Rabbits and Cavies, 76 pages. Printed in England. What you can feed if you must feed greens; with good illustrations.

Raising Earthworms for Profit, E.B. Shields. 128 pages. Best little book on earthworms I've read. Special chapter on worms and rabbits.

Official Guide Book of the American Rabbit Breeders Association, Inc. 200 pages of essential information for all rabbit raisers. Written by amateur volunteers, so much is difficult reading, but nevertheless a fine compilation of lore from years of experience. Free with membership at $7 per year. ARBA, 1925 S. Main St., Box 426, Dept. B, Bloomington, Ill. 61701. (Note: You need not have rabbits to join; nor does membership require any activity on your part.)

Rabbit Raising, Bob Bennett. 32 pages. Merit Badge booklet available in any Boy Scout supply store for 55 cents, or from Boy Scouts of America, North Brunswick, N.J. 08902. Aimed at youngsters, but concise book of tips with photos for anyone. The book that inspired this one.

Raising Rabbits, Farmers Bulletin No. 2131., United States Department of Agriculture. 24 pages. Send 15 cents to Superintendent of Documents, U.S. Government Printing Office, Washington, D.C. 20402. Dated but helpful. Prepared by Agricultural Research Service.

A Bibliography of the Domestic Rabbit. 22 pages. Bulletin 481 A, Cooperative Extension Service, Colorado State University, Fort Collins, Colo. 80521. Prepared by David D. Caveny and Howard L. Enos. A handy guide to semi-technical and technical articles; published in 1972.

The Purina Rabbit Book. 28 pages. Ralston Purina Company, Checkerboard Square, St. Louis, Mo. 63188. Free and a fine little booklet for meat producers.

Purina Rabbit Cage Plans. 6 pages. A free folder from Purina that shows how to build all-wire hutches with drawer-type nest boxes. Address above.

Rabbits. A Commercial Rabbit Raising Program. 78 pages. This is the best feed company booklet on raising meat rabbits that can be found. Free from Carnation Albers, Carnation Corp., Milling Division, 1700 Potter Ave., Kansas City, MO 64126

Raising Rabbits for Profit. 64 pages. Another fine free booklet from Carnation Albers. Address above.

Rabbits. An Albers Plan for Raising Rabbits. Still another excellent booklet for beginning meat producers. Free from Carnation Albers. Address above.

Domestic Rabbits: Diseases and Parasites, Agricultural Handbook No. 490. 65 cents from Superintendent of Documents, address above. This is a new booklet, published in 1976, based on USDA and Iowa State University research.

MAGAZINES

Domestic Rabbits. Official Publication of the American Rabbit Breeders Assn. Bi-monthly. Excellent articles although too few in each issue. Free with ARBA membership. Details, address above.
Rabbits The country's newest monthly rabbit magazine, from the publisher of *Countryside.* Monthly. $7 per year from *Rabbits,* Highway 19 East Waterloo, Wisconsin 53594.

NEWSLETTERS AND GUIDEBOOKS

For each recognized breed there is a newsletter and a guidebook that emanates from the specialty club devoted to the particular breed. Membership is required, at about $3 to $5 per year, but with additional benefits to be gained. Addresses for these breed specialty clubs, and also for hundreds of state, regional and local breeder associations, many of which also publish newsletters, can be found in the ARBA Yearbook, which is included in ARBA membership.

A WORD ABOUT THE AUTHOR

Bob Bennett breeds rabbits on 10 acres in Shelburne, Vermont, where he also raises vegetables and flowers. He was a public relations and advertising executive in Manhattan for a worldwide corporation in the animal health field before joining Garden Way Publishing as sales and marketing director in 1977.

Bob has freelanced many articles on a variety of subjects, especially rabbits, since 1971 when he founded *Domestic Rabbits* magazine, now the official publication of the ARBA. In 1976 he was elected to the ARBA Board of Directors. He has also served as editor of *Rabbits* magazine.

Suggested
Additional Reading

A good library is essential for the person or family raising animals or raising and storing food. No one can remember all of the information this requires, and a good library will provide it, at your fingertips. New ideas, techniques and theories are always being put forth, and the best way to keep up with them all is to keep your library up to date. There are many good books available; here are some that are excellent choices.

Tan Your Hide! Home Tanning Leathers & Furs, by Phyllis Hobson. Easy methods for the home tanner and fur skin worker. See description on p. 92 this book. 134 pp. illus. $6.95 + $1.75 P&H. Order #101-9.

The Canning, Freezing, Curing & Smoking of Meat, Fish & Game, by Wilbur F. Eastman Jr. An authoritative work on the art of home processing of meat, fish and game. Step-by-step instruction. 202 pp. illus. $5.95 + $1.75 P&H. Order #045-4.

The Family Cow, by Dirk van Loon. Covers cow buying, handling, housing, feeding, milking, caring, breeding, and calfing. Plus information on land use, hay and tools. 262 pp. illus. $8.95 + $1.75 P&H. Order #066-7

Raising Milk Goats the Modern Way, by Jerry Belanger. Complete up-to-date *how to* information for raising goats on a small to semi-commercial scale. 152 pp. photos & illus. $5.95 + $1.75 P&H. Order #062-4.

Raising Poultry the Modern Way, Leonard Mercia. In addition to complete *how-to* information for raising chickens, turkeys and waterfowl, you are given housing plans and source lists for supplies and equipment. 220 pp. illus. $7.95 + $1.75 P&H. Order #058-6

These books are available at your bookstore, lawn & garden center, or may be ordered directly from Garden Way Publishing, Dept. 4412 Schoolhouse Road, Pownal, Vt. 05261. Send for our free mail order catalog.

Equipment Suppliers

The following firms supply complete lines of rabbitry equipment. I have made purchases from them and know them to be reputable. Their equipment is of good quality. I cannot urge you too much to send for *all* these catalogs, study them and compare. They are indispensable to planning a rabbitry. Rabbit equipment suppliers are guileless, down-to-earth and honest.

Favorite Manufacturing Co., Box 176B, New Holland, Pa. 17557. Best hutch designs. Complete equipment line. Most progressive company in the business.

Michi-Crown, 6359 Wolverine Trail, Rt. 2B, Alger, Mich. Fifty cents for catalog, refunded with first order. Lots of handy items. Well worth four bits.

Glick Manufacturing Co., 420B East 9th St., Gilroy, Calif. 95020. Send $2 for "Commercial Rabbit Raisers Guide" with complete catalog.

Bass Equipment Co., RR No. 1-SB, Monett, Mo. 65708. Free catalog. Economy line of equipment. Lots of hints in catalog.

Valentine Equipment Co., 9706B South Industrial Drive, Bridgeview, Ill. 60455. Best catalog of al!, but costs a refundable $3. This is the Sears catalog of the rabbit business. Also includes other small animal, bird needs. You want it, they've got it.

Circle K Industries. Free catalog from Dept. 10, 21 N. 988 Pepper Road, Barrington, Ill. 60010. Finest quality equipment that costs more but is worth it in the long run.

New England Rabbitry Supply, RFD 3B, North Middleboro, Mass. 02346. Fifty cents but worth it for the disease control information and book list. Owner Joe Laura is a rabbit judge.

Mountain View Rabbitry Supply Co., Naples, Maine 04055.

Glossary

ANGORA — Rabbit with coat about 3 inches long. Raised for wool as well as meat.

BREED — Race of rabbits distinguished by looks, such as color, size, body type.

BREEDER — An adult rabbit used for propagation. Also, the person who keeps breeding rabbits, and breeds them in an effort to maintain and improve their special qualities. A breeder considers himself to be more than just a "raiser."

BUCK — A male rabbit.

BUCK TEETH — Protruding or crooked teeth; malloclusion; also called wolf teeth. Usually hereditary but sometimes caused by accident.

BUNNY — A cutesy term for rabbit. Babies are called bunnies for lack of another term, although some call the babies kits, even pups.

COBBY — Short, stocky body type.

CONDITION — State of general physical well-being, revealed by brightness of eye, sheen of coat, firmness of flesh, etc.

CREEP FEEDER — Special dispenser of feed for young rabbits that excludes doe.

DENSITY — Thickness of coat of fur.

DEWLAP — Fold of loose skin under the chin of does; normal in some breeds but a disqualification in others. Not a disease condition.

DISQUALIFICATION — A permanent physical defect. Disqualifications refer to show rabbits. These are listed in standard for each breed.

DOE — Female rabbit.

DWARF — Rabbit weighing no more than 3 pounds at maturity.

EAR CANKER — Scabby condition inside ear of rabbit; caused by mites.

ELIMINATION — A temporary defect that eliminates a rabbit from a show class. Eliminations are listed in each breed standard.

FALSE PREGNANCY — 17-day period when the doe cannot conceive. Brought on by sterile mating or other sexual stimulation.

FLY BACK — Fur which returns quickly to normal position when stroked "against the grain." Desirable fur condition in many normal-fur breeds.

GESTATION — Period of 28-34 days (usually 31) from mating to kindling.

GIANT — Rabbit weighing 12-16 pounds or more at maturity.

GUARD HAIR — Coarser, longer hair than underfur.

HOCK — First joint of hind leg, thickly padded with fur. What Thumper thumped.

HUTCH — Rabbit house; best are constructed only of wire and metal.

INBREEDING — Mating close relatives. Excellent practice when done wisely.

J-CLIPS — Special J-shaped metal clips used in hutch construction. Special pliers required for application.

JUNIOR — Rabbit under six months of age.

KINDLE — When a doe gives birth to a litter, she is said to kindle.

LINEBREEDING — Inbreeding for successive generations, generally mating "on a line" from and back to older specimens of the same family to capitalize on the specimen's special characteristics and to breed them into the "line."

MARKED — A rabbit with a fur pattern of two or more colors, such as the Tan or the Dutch.

MEDIUM BREED — Rabbit race with mature weight of 9-12 pounds.

MOLTING — Shedding fur.

NEST BOX — Provided to the doe on the 27th day after mating for birth of litter.

PAIR — Male and female to be mated to each other.

PALPATE — Pregnancy test. To feel for young in uterus of doe through abdomen.

PEDIGREE — Record of ancestry. Should include at least three generations.

PUREBRED — A specimen of a recognized breed from ancestors of that breed.

RACY — Slim, slender body type. A Belgian Hare is racy. A New Zealand is not.

REGISTRATION — Official examination and recording of rabbit pedigree by ARBA registrar. Only ARBA members may have rabbits registered.

REX — Rabbits with short, plush-like fur.

SATIN — Rabbits with transparent hair shaft providing extremely lustrous coat.

SENIOR — Rabbit over six months if of a breed that matures under 10 pounds. Over eight months if mature weight exceeds 10 pounds.

SNUFFLES — Respiratory disease, highly contagious, marked by nasal discharge.

SORE HOCKS — Ulcerated foot pads.

SPECIALTY CLUB — Rabbit club that specializes in a single breed.

STANDARD — Written physical description of a breed.

STRAIN — A family of rabbits within a breed, exhibiting distinguishing characteristics and passing them on from generation to generation; sometimes called a "line."

TATTOO — To mark ears with a permanent identification mark or number. Private number goes in left ear; registration number goes in right.

TEST-MATING — Returning doe to buck a week or 10 days after mating. If she complains she may be pregnant. Palpation is a surer method.

TRIO — A buck and two does of the same breed and perhaps the same variety.

TYPE — Body conformation.

VARIETY — A group within a breed; identified by color, e.g. New Zealand Red is a variety of the New Zealand breed.

WEANING — Separating the young from the doe, usually at six to eight weeks of age.

Plans for a Rabbit Shed

Here's how to build a shed for your rabbits from perforated steel angle iron which goes together like a child's construction set. Except for sheathing, no wood is used.

The angle iron I have found easy to use and find is called *Dexion*. An ordinary hex wrench and a Dexion cutter (which may be borrowed from the supplier) are all that is needed. These plans require a total of 176 feet of Dexion but you can easily reduce or enlarge them according to the number of cages you require. Measure carefully, then cut all the pieces. Another pair of hands will help when assembling the basic frame.

Galvanized sheet metal was used for dropping boards. A good pitch front to back is necessary so droppings will roll to the rear and fall to the ground. Make sure you leave enough room in front between the cage bottom and the dropping pan to use a scraper or hoe occasionally.

Because Dexion is steel, it does not rot in contact with the ground. It can be bolted to footings or treated wooden members (such as railroad ties, perhaps buried underground.) Bolt *exterior grade plywood* to the framing and finish to your liking (cedar shingles, paint, rough-cut lumber, etc.)

The roof should be covered with plywood and finished with shingles to assure water-tightness. It's a good idea to provide an overhang in front (as shown in photo on page 46) to help keep you dry in the rain while tending your rabbits and also to keep the sun off the animals.

Cleanout panels in back, hinged 18 inches off the ground, are helpful in cleaning the droppings from beneath the cages. A roll-up canvas in front further helps protect the cages from inclement weather.

These plans are only meant as a guide to help you along. Specific instructions can only relate to specific installations; common sense is your best guide. Should you have a problem with them, please feel welcome to contact me at One Governor's Lane, Shelburne VT 05482.

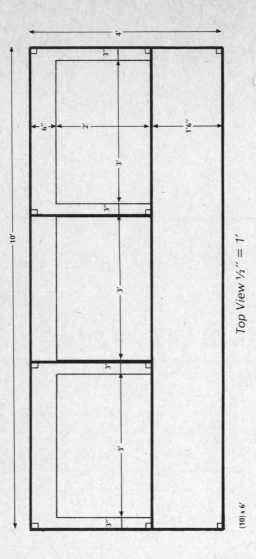

Top View ½″ = 1′

(10) x 6′

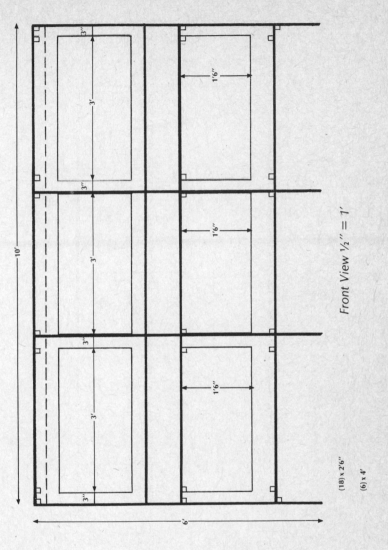

Front View ½" = 1'

(18) x 2'6"

(6) x 4'

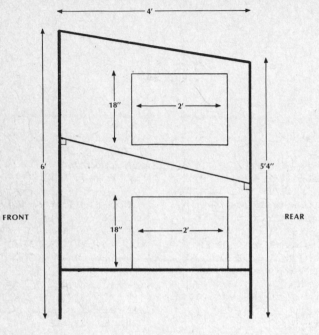

End View ½" = 1'

Index